RETHINKING LIFE

The GUIDEBOOK for RECREATING YOUR LIFE and WINNING the GAME

Michelle Laura Romero

MICHELLE LAURA ROMERO

RETHINKING LIFE

The GUIDEBOOK for RECREATING YOUR LIFE and WINNING the GAME

Copyright 2018 by Michelle Laura Romero

The author of this book does not dispense financial or medical advice or prescribe the use of any technique as a form of investing or treatment without the consultation of a financial advisor or physician. The intent of the author is only to offer information of a general nature to assist you in your quest for financial independence and overall well-being. In the event you use any of the information in this book for yourself, the author and the publisher assume no responsibility for your actions.

Published by: Kindle Direct Publishing

ISBN 9781726846509

Contents

Dedication

This book is dedicated to my beloved sons, Ryan, Kyle 'Schodd', Mayrshtu', and Tsayqmoh who continue to inspire me everyday through their innocence and innate wisdom. Be inspired my sons; allow your inner light to guide you through life, so that you may fulfill your destiny. My love for you is as infinite as your possibilities.

Prologue

Welcome to the game of your life and a world of everlasting abundance. This world was created out of the purest energy source by the highest power and has been expanding from the very beginning of time by way of collective consciousness. All riches necessary within the world were provided at the inception, and then expansion brought about flourishing diversity in life. The world was pure.

Our realm was created as a way for the Originator to experience the physicality and emotionality as a being within the living world. Through free will and the natural laws our species have been discovering the delicate balance that was created for us and is shaped by us with every thought and action of our people. The wisest among of us will choose to retain the ability to reproduce and nurture physically, mentally, and emotionally virile beings to keep the world in balance with our Creator's intentions. The game begins with us.

However, unbeknownst to the populace the world had been created in duality. The people slowly allowed their emotions to take over their certainty. Although, they had found great fruitfulness and joy in their world, in that joy was fear. The idea that the world and all of its richness could be taken from them, uncertainty ensued. Those thoughts allowed a darkness to come, and it has remained.

Now it is here, residing since that time began. The world has been increasingly depleted of vital energy by an unseen force both internally and externally that have slowly overtaken and shifted the minds of the unsuspecting populace. The goal of those who understand the power remains: to harvest energy and deplete the planet and its sentient beings of their once rich lives and home planet. What once was a world of enlightened gods has now become an energetic feeding ground of despair and enslavement.

In this creation you call life, you are your savior. A hero avatar, you have been granted a unique gift by the Source. This Source wisdom remains inside of you as your internal guide through the now confused energetic forces in this realm. You may already be aware of your abilities, or they may have been hidden deep inside of you through mind programming, distraction, or genetic alteration.

Be aware that there are those in this game who will never recover their purpose during this lifetime. They are caught up in the distractions of the game. They will cycle through until they are open and ready for the knowledge that has been concealed from their minds. Your objective is to rediscover the power already within you and complete the game. Only then can you return to the inception and be among the masters.

Throughout your journey, your wisdom, spirituality, and self-knowingness will be challenged at every turn. The obstacles, which have been chosen for you, include *everlasting life*, the *quest for riches*, *choosing alliances*, *increased health*, *strategy*, and *leveling-up* on your mission. By the end of the challenge, you will not only need to master each obstacle in which you have been presented, but you must also prepare for unforeseen challenges that may arise on your journey. You must succeed so that you may return on your path prepared to move forward with your intended destiny. As you move forward toward simplicity, your path, which has been your innate gift since birth, will become clear once again. Learn from the challenges while *rethinking life*.

Imagine a world in which peace returns to the land, abundance flows from every corner, and the people reign united from their highest potential. The apex will be the time of self-actualization among the human beings. Are you ready to learn the principles and prepared to challenge what you thought you knew about life?

Every action, whether positive or negative, creates definite and definable reactions. The world has been shaped in all ways by the beings that have resided here, so be cautious of your own intentions and deeds as you move forward and navigate your journey. You are producing your current reality. How can life and all of its aspects seem to be so flawless for some and so burdensome for others?

No one is free from the lessons of life. The lessons come when redirection is necessary to remain on the path, and where wisdom is most prevalently learned. Think of a child who is misbehaving. First, the parent gives a word of redirection. If the child does not oblige, the parent becomes more direct, perhaps tapping the child on the shoulder or raising their voice. Again, if the child does not stop, the parent takes the next step — time-out, spanking, withholding a toy. If the lessons are not being heard, then they become louder and harsher. Listen to the whispers in life, or face the consequences. Those that seem always to be winning at the game of life are living in alignment with natural laws and according to the timeless principles of success.

These principles of success have been handed down from generation to generation through the noblest, most elite, and successful families. To them, the knowledge has become second nature and is used for conquering obstacles that seem impossible to most. Those less fortunate and ignorant of the success principles have historically retained few options. Most remain impoverished.

Then there are those players with insight and drive who push past the social norms to create a new destiny for themselves by uncovering and emulating the winning principles of the elite. Acquiring the fundamental skills and practicing them purposely on a daily basis will propel the most driven player in the desired direction.

We are going to break down the principles into their simplest forms, so that you may step-by-step create the successful life you have always desired. The cycles of poverty, poor health, failed relationships, self-destruction, and endless unconscious patterns that you have been living can be a thing of the past. You are going to be the change for yourself, your community, your family, and for generations to follow.

A word of caution for the players in this game: play the game with purity of heart, integrity, and honesty. *You are already in the game.* Now it is time to become its master. Your honor will be tested, your heart torn, be true to yourself until the very end.

RETHINKING LIFE

The GUIDEBOOK for RECREATING YOUR LIFE and WINNING the GAME

Forward with **David J. Console**

If you were playing a computerized game with only *one avatar life*, how would you play? Would it be with care, purpose, and intention? Our lives are the most important game we will ever play, but too many of us are playing carelessly. To win one must plan, strategize, assess, reassess, and move forward with intention. The game has changed and so must our strategy. Our objective is to master the missions and surpass obstacles within our path. Do more than just finish the game; win it!

As a colleague of Michelle Laura Romero's for over a decade we have worked closely and shared many intellectual and creative perspectives on the many facets of life, health, family, and money. When faced with challenging situations, Michelle shares her practical psychological approaches to regain clarity of thinking, physical collectiveness, solution-based perspectives, as well as action plans to move forward in the face of life's obstacles.

The tenacity, resilience, and self-awareness of the author have come by learning from life's storms, coming out the other side even more prepared to win. Read further and Michelle will outline how to navigate life and win the "game." As a mother of four young men, manager of an award-winning Arizona resort casino, author, and speaker, Michelle teaches her audience that you cannot control the wind, but you can control your sails. I am proud and honored to be part of bringing this important information to light and excited to dive even deeper into the mind of this intriguing teacher.

Prepare for your journey by first becoming your own hero. The guidebook is in your hands. Learn the principles of creating the life you were meant to lead. Outlined are instructions for navigating your *quest for riches*, choosing the correct *alliances* along your journey, *increasing your health* and longevity as well as *navigating your plan* and *leveling-up* along the way, all while defining *your purpose*.

Chapter 1

The Principles and Mechanics of Winning

Wisdom is the essential basis of greatness.

- Wallace D. Wattles

Real life's complexities can be compared to the complexities of a computerized program, a role-playing video game. Imagine you in your life being a heroic game character. You are navigating your way through progressively more complex challenging levels of the game within your life. Your health is optimal, your outlook positive, you are unscathed and excited about the journey ahead of you. The only drawback is that unlike a game, there are no extra lives, no spare players. Now you must play the game even more cautiously. You have one life; it's your only shot at winning the game. Welcome to your own personal journey through life.

In this life, you have been given one chance to collect the necessary gold coins, learn the appropriate skills, acquire supplies, build a suitable shelter, and choose the right allies, all while avoiding the pitfalls, villains, dangers, and distractions that could be the end of you. The game is a parallel of your own life. The possibilities that lie ahead are endless. Will you win, or will you manifest your own demise? Every game, as well as life, can begin easily enough. As you progress, the levels become more difficult and the challenges require more wisdom. This game will require goal setting, time management, life experience, and keen observation skills to spot the dangers that lie ahead of you.

What if I handed you a guide, a cheat book for the game? Wouldn't that help you navigate your way through the obstacles? You still have to play the game, but it would help you avoid some critical mistakes along your journey. The guidebook is what you have in your hands right now. Merely follow the cheats along the way and see how much simpler the game becomes.

This analogy of real life and the video game simulation flashed into my mind as a vision while I returned home from taking my eldest son to work one spring day. He was my firstborn, Ryan, a then eighteen-year-old young man finding his way in life and at the same time seeking independence from his family. I was a mother who was not quite sure how to allow his freedom while also ensuring that I instill the principles he must learn and know to succeed. He would define his course while I would remain a guide. We were at a crossroads in our relationship and a transition in our lives, game-changer.

The correlation flashed in my mind's eye. Yes, of course! Ryan knew how to conquer video games better than anyone I had ever known. He had been playing since he could hold a controller. This parallel was going to be the bridge that we needed to relate to one another and allow the principles to flow between us. Life is like an adventure video game! I felt my excitement and anticipation to share my epiphany. When I returned later that afternoon to pick Ryan up from work, I quickly relayed the principles to him.

Now, these principles have been handed on to you. Follow them carefully in your own life. They are simple but take self-discipline to master. The further you get into the game the more you will master the necessary skills and the better you will become. Stay your course, outline your objectives for winning, and most of all be true to yourself. You decide when you have won, and only you will know how badly you want to win. Best of luck on your journey.

Chapter 2

One Life, One Avatar

One Life. Just one. Why aren't we running like we are on fire towards our wildest dreams?

- Author unknown

Quite obvious to most players, *One Life, One Avatar* is a key principle to winning any game, but dire to the game you call life. The consequences of which cannot be ignored. You have been given *one life, one avatar* to accomplish your objectives. You must not only possess a strong will to live, but an unwavering commitment to persevere through the darkest trials and temptations. There are numerous missions to master before reaching your final destination. This game matters, not only to us, but it has eternal consequences for the future. You must play each mission intelligently, cautiously, and with definite purpose. If not, it is simply GAME OVER.

As I explained this principle to Ryan, we sat in our vehicle at a red streetlight in a bustling intersection of Metropolitan Phoenix, Arizona where hundreds of people cross the streets throughout the day. The crosswalk sign flashed DO NOT WALK when a disheveled older gentleman seemingly lost in his thoughts began to make his way into the crosswalk. I looked at Ryan to see if he noticed the impending disaster. The pedestrian slowly made his move and was about halfway to the other side of the busy intersection when the light for the truck directly in front of him changed to a green arrow. The truck began to pull-forward when at the last minute the driver noticed the gentleman crossing. He had formerly been hidden behind another vehicle that pulled up too far into the crosswalk. The truck had to slam on its brakes to avoid hitting the unwise cross-walker. The pedestrian broke the number one critical principle, *One Life, One Avatar* and was almost taken out of the game right in front of us. It was a serendipitous moment for both Ryan and myself.

That was it! I explained to Ryan, that is the fundamental principle of life. The oblivious pedestrian almost took himself out of the game by foolishly crossing the street when it clearly said, "DO NOT WALK." I explained to Ryan that not everyone is good at the game. Just like with his video games, which he's extremely proficient, it takes skill to "level-up" and ultimately win this undertaking.

Can you think of a time when you or someone you knew was almost taken out of the game due to carelessness? We have all had these moments, which were warning signs of our fragile existence in life. They represent a time of *rethinking* our current position within the game. A personal reminder of the *One Life, One Avatar* principle that had been told many times in my family was that of my older sister, Heather, who had been taken from us in a car accident during the winter of 1996. She was a twenty-year-old college junior; I was eighteen in my first year at the university.

Over two decades later, as a mother of four, I had gained the insight and an internal knowing that I did not want my children to grow up thinking that "accidents just happen." Accidents do not just happen; they are a consequence of our choices or the choices of another. It is easy for us to blame situations or other people for the positions we find our lives and ourselves. But, how often do we look at our actions for the results we obtain? I dare say, not as often as we should. Unfortunately, some decisions have dire and long-lasting consequences. This was one example among the many.

I made a conscious choice to explain to all of my boys, who ranged in ages at that time from eighteen to two years old, that Aunt Heather was not careful enough when she was driving and the conditions in which she chose to drive, and that is why she was not with us today. She rolled the dice as so many of us do and it did not work out in her favor. She lost the game.

Heather was a straight-A student at a prestigious private college in Alma, Michigan when she left us. My sister was wise beyond her years and had a bright future, but it did not change the reality of what happened. As she had done so many weekends before, Heather was on her way home from college to see my parents and her longtime boyfriend. The difference on this visit was that black ice had formed on the road. Heather would hit the patch of black ice, and her vehicle would slide into the oncoming traffic, killing her instantly.

This event changed not only her life by ending it, but it also changed the life of the man that hit her, and all of those that knew and loved Heather. My own life would never be the same. I was determined not to let this event destroy me as it had done to other members of the family. Since I could make my own choices in life, I would choose to ripple this event and change future generations in our family by rewriting the story I told myself about this misfortunate event.

Because my parents were understandable inconsolable over the realization of my sister's passing, I hesitantly volunteered to identify her body that night in the hospital. She was just as I remembered her. Besides one little scratch on her face, she looked flawless, which made it indescribably difficult to understand how she could be gone. I grew as a person at that moment, standing there with Heather in her now peaceful state knowing that utter confusion was just outside those doors. I hesitated to move from her side knowing that I would be leaving her for nearly the last time and entering into a life of chaos without my only beloved sibling, but there was no choice. The world was going to move forward with or without us. It changed the trajectory of my path in life. I knew I had to have a greater purpose and although it would not be without many more harsh life lessons, I would reach for my fullest potential for Heather and for myself. *One life, one avatar* was lost that day; now it was my responsibility to win the game for both of us.

The coping methods, to which we tend to default when emotional and tragic events occur, keep us from taking an honest look at missteps and changing the trajectory of the future in a positive direction. Do not allow the emotionality of these events to take over your life. Moving on is a choice. Living was a privilege my sister did not have after that day, but destroying two lives over the circumstances would be even more of a waste. Taking a realistic look at what led to the passing of my sister allowed me a more wise explanation than an "accident," which in my mind creates a victim outlook and no recourse or possibility for other results for anyone in the future. She was not a victim in her passing. If we want to win the game we have to discard the victim mentality from our perception.

The same goes for smoking, drinking, drugs, violence, pornography, rolling the dice, overeating, and risky sexual behavior. All of which are distractions from winning and will bring down your life energy. Their use has the potential for shortening your life with no foreseeable benefits or progression within the game. Do we want to live a life in which we need to escape, or create the life in which we want to live? These seemingly enjoyable additives for some are mere distractions to take you out of your full game potential.

Be aware that much more experienced players with alternative motives have introduced these distractors into society with hopes of personal gain for themselves. The financial growth they obtain from such diversions is used to propel these strategic players into much higher levels of their own game. Do not get their game confused with your own, and do not believe that all of the players within the game have your best interests in mind. It is a single player's game with allies at best, and at worst it is cutthroat and ruthless. Be wise, be skillful.

Be aware, suicide, depression, emotional darkness, emotional triggers, self-harming behaviors are signs of dangerously low energy levels. Assessments must be made in every area of life when this occurs. Where is the imbalance occurring in your life? Identify the instability and implement the life principles you will be learning when these symptoms occur. You must know your reason for moving forward in the game. What is your why? Do you want a family? Do you want to meet your great-grandchildren one day? Are you looking forward to seeing the world in your old age? Dreams are not meant just for children. A vision for the future and a plan for getting there must be put into place.

When one becomes unbalanced, changes must be implemented immediately to avoid a downward spiral that would result in detrimental decisions and outcomes. The principles of life tell us that what goes up must come down. The lowest point will follow the highest point in life, and then the progression begins again. The past cannot be redone, and the future is unwritten. All things are possible in your mind and this game. You are creating your destiny and fulfilling the potential you create in your own life.

Many lives ended tragically before the players achieved self-fulfillment. Why was this? Fundamentally, the players did not understand the principles of life and the rule of *One Life, One Avatar*. The harsh reality is that if you are not alive and well physically and emotionally you cannot play the game optimally, which makes it impossible to win. Winning is everything. You can make a lot of mistakes with the other principles and still recover, but *One Life, One Avatar* is final and must be upheld. Winning was never promised and not meant to be easy, but our mission remains. Do you have the courage, the determination, the intellect, and the insight to stay in the game?

Your Avatar Life

➢ **Where do you feel your life currently out of balance (finances, relationships, health, spirituality, individuality, purpose, etc.)?**

- _____

- _____

- _____

➢ **What events/emotions are you distracting yourself from?**

- _____

- _____

- _____

➢ **What are you distracting yourself with (alcohol, food, television, etc.)?**

- _____

- _____

- _____

➢ **What steps do you need to take to improve your outcome in the game? How are you going to change directions?**

- _____

- _____

- _____

Chapter 3

Quest for Riches

Be fearful when others are greedy. Be greedy when others are fearful.

- Warren Buffett

In this journey of life, our heroic and ideal self will come across many impending distractions related to wealth building. Are you willing to navigate these obstacles to acquire the necessary principles to build your empire? You have been programmed for instant gratification since the beginning of the game. It is time to go deeper into this level past the golden idols, diamonds and rubies, and artifacts to overcome over-spending and unrefined money skills. The key players misguided your predecessors and enslaved them all with consumer debt. You have limited time to win back your power, save your future, and set your people free. It is time to begin.

During this time of credit invasion, it is difficult to discern who is wealthy from those that only appear wealthy. Cash has been replaced by plastic in order to increase consumer spending. Do not be blinded by the vehicles, gadgets, and accessories of other players. Wise players know these items were purchased on credit and the enslaved owners are living paycheck to paycheck. One small disaster, one emergency, a broken bone, and the glass house will crumble. This illusion of wealth can take even the most skilled player off course. It is imperative to think of the bigger picture in such circumstances. Would you like the options someone who is financially secure retains, or do you want to live paycheck to paycheck until the grave? To determine your score at this level of the game subtract your debts from your assets. The difference is your net worth. Your score may be positive or negative, but do not be afraid. This mission can be mastered utilizing a few key principles.

Principle One: Credit Is a Construct, Debt Is Self-Imposed Slavery

Those that have followed historical trends are reminded that there is an ebb and flow to the financial sector. The powers that be are pulling strings behind the scenes causing impulse reactions from the unsuspecting population. We are going to put ourselves in a proactive position of power to limit the potentially destructive nature of the markets. Cash is the master of this level; credit is the enemy. It is time to create personal wealth and stop lining the pockets of the overlords with high-interest rate payments. From this point forward consumer credit is off limits.

It is important to take the lessons from those that we observed winning as well as those we noticed losing in our own lives. Although my family did not directly discuss financial matters with me, I was keenly aware of the winners in my family. My maternal grandfather Harold came from Germany when he was a boy. He was raised on the family farm and became a factory worker.

He and my grandmother Eleanor, who was also raised in the depression, worked hard and they worked smart.

Harold, whom I did not realize was not my natural grandfather until much later in life, married my grandmother against his own mother's wishes. He had taken on a lot when he married my grandmother who had been abandoned with four young children by my mother's father. Harold was my grandfather and loved us like his own. With one sentence and his life experience being raised in the depression, my grandfather shaped my view on money. He told me, "If you want something, save for it and pay cash." I never forgot those important words, although it did take nearly twenty years for me to fully understand and apply what he had shared with me that day.

My grandparents had been unknowingly instilled in their depression era youth with key winning factors that helped them win the game monetarily. Hardship during their childhoods propelled them forward light years ahead in the game. In my grandparent's garages were always well cared-for, and in my young view, like-new vehicles. Their modest mid-century modern home had been built for cash and with my grandfather's own hands. They had periodically owned investment properties, oil wells, and certainly had other financial investments. They diversified and had a plan for their money. They vacationed, went out frequently with friends, and enjoyed each other and their lives. They chose to delay instant gratification and establish themselves in order to create an amazing life for themselves and their family. Harold and Eleanor understood and applied the fundamental principle of winning with a debt-free life.

Tabulate Your Consumer Debts

➢ **Department Store Credit Card**   **$2.500**

➢ _____

➢ _____

➢ _____

➢ _____

➢ _____

➢ _____

➢ _____

➢ _____

➢ _____

➢ _____

The Price of Freedom $_____

Principle Two: Collecting Golden Coins

After acknowledging that you will never be financially stable or debt-free by constantly re-entering the debt cycle you can begin to take necessary precautions that will help offset household emergencies. This wise move puts winners in a more powerful frame of mind versus a reactive stressful state of mind. You cannot continue to keep putting out fires.

Instead, you will plan to win. A wise hero knows that unexpected expenses can put a halt to progress within the game and instinctively saves for such events. To begin, quickly stock up a $1,000 emergency savings account. Eventually, you will hold a minimum 6-months of reserve as well as a vehicle fund after all consumer debts have been repaid. Emergency savings is a pivotal turning point in the game and must be completed before beginning the next principle.

How do I calculate the amount that I should have in my 6-Month Emergency Reserve?

Formula:

Monthly Household Expenses x 6-Months =

6-Month Emergency Reserve

Example: $2,700 x 6 = $16,200 Emergency Reserve

Principle Three: Knowing Where Your Life Energy Is Flowing

Without a financial plan, it is almost impossible to succeed at the game. Your time is equivalent to the price you accept for your service. This means time spent away from your family, your personal goals, your pastimes, and ultimately your life. What is your time worth? How much of your life do you trade away to creditors? It is time to lay out your plan with a written monthly budget. Know how much energy you have to extend to sustain and cut ALL extras until you pay off your creditors. You have your own goals to reach on your journey. It is time to take back your life energy and redistribute the gold. What matters to you most, the present or the possibilities? This level can be accomplished quickly and must be sustained until the completion of the game.

Your first objective is to write an all-inclusive itemized monthly budget for your household, which will serve as a quick reference guideline and assist with the subsequent building of your yearly budget. There should be no surprises on your monthly budget. Things like holidays, birthdays, graduations, oil changes, home maintenance, and car registration are anticipated expenses and should be added to the budget.

From this point, you will continue to build your actual monthly expenses month-by-month for the entire year in a weekly or bi-weekly manner depending on how you are paid by your employer. Be sure to include any yearly, one-time, or periodic payments. Be true to your spending; remember that you are not fooling anyone. If you want real change to happen in your life be truthful with yourself about your circumstances. Are you ready to look honestly at your spending habits? If you are, it will change your life. You are the hero in this game; no one is going to save you except yourself.

Sample Monthly Household Base Budget:

Base Monthly Expenses

1	Childcare	$600	
1	Grocery	$600	
1	Gas	$80	
1	Mortgage	$801	
15	Electric	$80	(Average)
15	Cable	$73.63	
15	Phone	$57	
15	Water	$120	(Average)
25	Auto Insurance	$94.88	
	Total Base Expenses	$2,506.51	

Other

Term Life Insurance	$24	($71.12 Quarterly)
Car Registration	$14	($168 Yearly - August)
Total Other Expenses	$38	

Total Monthly Expenses	$2,544.51	(Base + Other Expenses)
6-Month Emergency Fund	$15,267.06	($2,544.51 x 6 months)

Use the space below to calculate the amount of your 6-month Emergency Reserve:

$_____ **Total Monthly Household Expenses X 6-Months =**

$_____ **6-Month Emergency Reserve Goal**

How much does it cost you to live everyday?

➢ **Example:**

$2,544.51 Total Monthly Expenses / 30 Days in the Month =

$84.82 Per Day to Sustain the Household

➢ **Calculate:**

$_____ **Total Monthly Expenses / # Days in the Month =**

$_____**Per Day**

Now think about how much your household earns each day and decide, what is your life energy worth?

Principle Four: Building Your Legacy

You have made it this far on your mission, now to address your objectives toward wealth building. To proceed in the game and reach the final phases of freedom and independence from those who understand the structuring of power it is necessary to break the familial cycle. The wealthy have held these principles secret from the commoners, but in our observations, we can surmise that investing in the future and educating the next generation undermines their agenda.

As many generations before, our parents, grandparents, and great-grandparents have been very tight-lipped on yearly salary, monthly expenses, and retirement savings. Considered a social taboo in many families and cultures, this has been a dangerous practice and one that has not served us well. Communication occurs much more intentionally among wealthy families. To handle wealth when it enters our lives, we must have a plan to obtain and facilitate the growth of our assets.

More and more employers in modern society provide a 401K for their employees as well as an employer match incentive. Therefore, if you are an employee who assigns 10% of your pre-tax salary to your 401K, then your employer would match up to 5%. Some employers are now providing a Roth 401K, in which you allocate after-tax funds into your investment account. When available, it is prudent to choose a Roth-401K over a traditional 401K. Either way, the most crucial advice for investing is to save early and save often when investing for retirement. Strive to allocate

15%-20% of your annual salary into investments with proven long-term high rates of return toward your future. Always pay yourself first, automatically whenever possible. A caution for the wise player in this game: DO NOT cash out your 401K when you change employers, and DO NOT take a loan against your 401K for any reason. Doing so will lead to losing precious compounding interest time in the investment game. When you leave an employer, instead choose to "roll-over" your investments with another investment broker. We have discussed your 6-month Emergency Reserve, but we will also consider other options and proactive approaches for avoiding loans against retirement accounts.

The purpose of a retirement account is to build enough wealth in your portfolio to sustain your household off of the interest it creates on an annual basis. It is a common misconception that the gross amount in the account is to be withdrawn or diminished to sustain the individual, but this is false and should be avoided.

Many financial difficulties can be prevented with proper planning. How many times in your life have you seen families ruined by lack of financial planning? Aging is unavoidable, illness is a reality for most in our society, death is inevitable. Why is it that many families still experience financial devastation during these times? In your game, it does not have to be that way. You are the decision maker, the hero. These are not tools exclusively for the wealthy. The acquisition of an inexpensive Term Life Insurance Policy, Long and Short-Term Disability Insurance (often offered by employers), as well as having a Will, Power of Attorney, and Trust in place will not only save time and money but also alleviate unnecessary stresses. These tools in your arsenal are a necessity. Knowing you and your family are taken care of during difficult times will take these pressures off of your subconscious mind. And, when the mind is at ease so is the body.

Planning for Your Future

- ➢ **Retirement Accounts (401K, Roth 401K, IRA, Roth IRA, etc.)**

  - _____

  - _____

- ➢ **Term Life Insurance Policy(ies)**

  - _____

  - _____

- ➢ **Long and Short Term Disability Insurance**

  - _____

  - _____

- ➢ **Will, Power of Attorney, Trust**

  - _____

  - _____

  - _____

Principle Five: Headquarters, Creating the Safe House

It is no secret that the winners of this game are landowners. The hierarchy remains: the royals, the nobles, and the peasants. Paying monthly assessments to the nobles for a property does not lead to wealth building. It is necessary to jump the hierarchy by understanding and applying the principles in this section. To acquire a headquarters via land ownership be advised that additional assessments must be made. These include: determining what minimum living requirements are necessary for your comfort, as well as determining a safe level of financial risk that would be appropriate based on your current life style and income. Be aware that a mortgage broker, mortgage lender, or banker's pre-approval amount is typically a higher amount than most potential homeowners actually need or should be taking on. Wise players choose to live far below their means.

Many unsuspecting homeowners have fallen into the trap of purchasing beyond their means, also called house poor. Other traps players fall into are buying homes with square footage much higher than necessary, which means more money to furnish, heat, and cool a larger dwelling. What about the idea of purchasing homes with additional bedrooms for relatives who visit once or twice a year? Again, that means accounting for additional furnishings, heating/cooling, higher taxes, and more upkeep and maintenance. A wise player purchases what they need to sustain themselves and their immediate family to win the game. It is unwise to take players into account who do not directly contribute to your homestead.

Gracious guests are grateful for any accommodations that a host may offer. There are many lessons to learn within the game.

Learn the lessons of the past. Like millions of homeowners in the early 2000's, my family experienced a financial wake-up call with a foreclosure. At the time we felt untouchable as many did, with great jobs, a newly built house with a conventional loan and nearly $200,000 in equity, but we also held student loans, car loans, and credit card debt. We felt entitled to vacations and purchased on a whim. Our home was a huge financial risk to us because of how much debt we had accumulated.

We eventually realized our dream home was far too big for our family and took up way too much of our precious downtime to upkeep, so we half-heartedly put it for sale on the market. Unfortunately, we were ignorant of the vast amounts of subprime mortgage loans that had been lent out to homeowners. We never did get ahead of the market crash. Every time we lowered our asking price, the market sunk further and further. Until finally we knew it was over. The mortgage aside, we had always stayed current with our consumer debts. Regardless, we walked away and the house eventually went back to the bank, but not without taking some of our vital life energy with it.

Shortly after, the phone calls began. It all felt familiar, the harassment, the threats. After the dust had settled, I realized that this was a pattern set up during my childhood. Navigating your way through life means often reflecting on the past to identify patterns of behavior and reoccurring cycles, and then taking purposeful action to prevent inflicting these same missteps upon your future.

I recognized that my family had gone through a very similar situation when I was in high school. My father had taken us on vacation along the East Coast after relocating our family to open a satellite operation for the company he had worked for the last eighteen years. When we returned from our trip, my father's supervisor had said that he had abandoned his job. That was not the case, but my father lost his job that day. The betrayal hurt my father to the core and nearly ruined our family financially and emotionally. My sister and I were in high school and now dealing with adult problems. The phone would ring multiple times a day, bill collectors, asking for my father. We would pretend he was not home, and also let them know that we did not know when he would return. It became a norm to hear from bill collectors, and now, in my adult life, I had repeated the same cycle. It was unacceptable to me.

I made a conscious decision during that time: the cycle would stop with me. I recognized that the down market was the time wealth was built, not at the top. At the lowest point in the market, I purchased another home and vowed to forego all emotional ties to real estate. At that time, I gained valuable insight into the financial game. I sold my next home on the upswing of the market and downsized again, which allowed me to allocate the remaining funds into a 6-month emergency reserve, a vehicle fund, and left me retaining a smaller and lower risk mortgage. The savings in utilities and financial security meant I could level-up in the game, pay off the mortgage within a few years and go even deeper into the game. It allowed me time to enjoy my family, time to dream again, and the financial freedom to make those dreams happen.

Your mission in real estate is to buy low, sell high, strategically downsize, purchase in a desirable location, and pay off your mortgage as quickly as possible. The current trend is toward renting as a way to ease financial tensions on a short-term basis, which is a trend of the poor. As a rule, housing prices will continue to increase with only periodic dips. DO NOT get caught in the rental trap. Yes, the owner takes the financial hits of repairs and responsibilities, but with ZERO debt and an emergency reserve, home ownership allows for huge wins on your journey.

As home prices continue to rise, so do rental prices. The subprime mortgage crisis put fear into players who are now reluctant to enter the real estate game. They feel renting is a lower risk venture which allows the freedom to move without the strings of responsibility, but they are missing out on the big picture. Rent only for the short-term when getting established, and rent far below your means to save for a down payment on a conventional short-term loan. A short-term mortgage retains a consistent monthly payment with the long-term benefits of a payoff and built-in equity. Rental prices will continue to rise and are a never-ending liability against your assets, which in turn lowers your net worth.

Pay off your mortgage as quickly as possible after paying off all consumer debt. When first beginning your real estate climb I advise a fixed interest rate conventional loan with the lowest terms you can secure, 10-15 years preferably. A common fallacy given to the masses is that homeownership with a mortgage comes with tax benefits. DO NOT fall for the tax benefits of a mortgage, which continue to be propaganda used to fleece the purchaser of nearly the same amount that they purchased for the home. You will never recoup the amount of interest paid to your mortgage company in your tax return. Work the game; do not let it work you. Systems of manipulation have been put in place to hypnotize the unsuspecting players. Mortgages are a risk and one that a knowledgeable player finds undesirable. A mortgage-free property is an extremely low-risk asset, as well as fulfilling the basic need of shelter. A hero's goal is to leave a legacy for their family through the accumulation of diverse investments.

For young people at the beginning of their game, it is a good idea to remain with your parents and save a proper down payment on an affordable starter-home or condominium. Your first property could later be used as a rental property providing residual income after you become more experienced in the game. Give yourself a tight deadline and stick with it. Hitting goals creates increased energy resulting in even more momentum. Play two steps ahead or more in the game. Anticipate your next move. The planner is rewarded on this journey.

Sample Goal for the Novice Player:

$10,000 saved per year x 4 years living with parents =

$30,000 down payment + $10,000 Emergency Fund

The skilled forces behind the housing industry have been programming their front men on directing the unknowing masses into low down payments and long-term loans. Then, when a home attains equity, those same front men are trained to encourage the homeowner to take out the equity in the form of another interest-bearing loan. Again, if the payment of the first mortgage and the home equity loan become too high the consumer is again persuaded, but this time to refinance the loans into one payment and an even longer-term loan.

The average player in this game does not realize that being mortgage-free is possible for them. We have been misled through strategic propaganda and familial cycles to put ourselves into financial ruin, which only benefits other players in the game. It is time to take back our power on this journey and use it to build our wealth.

The elite and the nobles in this quest are not like the average novice player. The wealthy have been taught to purchase and invest in things that create even more wealth, while the unprepared poor are programmed to spend their money on consumerism and items with depreciating value. The wealthy use education as a strategic tool to further their financial success, while the poor and middle-class take a less practical approach applied without a definitive plan. If you want to win you have to think outside of the norm and rethink what you have been taught. It is time to awaken to your fullest potential.

Planning for Your Safe House

➢ **Location, Location, Location (Choose the smallest home fitting your requirements in the best neighborhood and city you can afford.)**

- _____

- _____

- _____

➢ **Minimum Requirements for Housing (Sq. Footage, # Bedrooms, etc.)**

- _____

- _____

- _____

- _____

- _____

- _____

➢ **Desired Price Range based on a 10-15 year Conventional Mortgage with 20% Down Payment.**

- **(10 yr.)** _____

- **(15 yr.)** _____

➢ **Accelerated Payoff Goal, which will be less than the 10-15 year Mortgage**

- _____

Chapter 4

Choose Alliances Wisely

If you fail to plan, you are planning to fail.

- Benjamin Franklin

Each person is on their own mission and playing at a different level based on experience, wisdom, and goals. You have to assess where you are in the challenge and where you want to be. It's best to work backwards. What are the results you are seeking by the end of the game? Then, work back from that point to place yourself in the present moment. You must know yourself to win your mission. If not, you will be letting other players throw you off course that will undoubtedly determine your fate based on their own journey. It could take years to overcome these mistakes. Choose wisely and be strong in your convictions.

Not every person deserves the right to be your ally. You must be keenly aware of people's motives, patterns of behavior, and their desire for personal growth or lack there of. You must also be mindful of the distractors. Never cloud your judgment with alcohol or other mind-altering substances when getting to know someone; you will never see a person's true nature under such circumstances. A shill can hide under such guises and lead you astray.

Time wasters and distractors will bring you down with temptation in the form of drugs, alcohol, dysfunction, and sedentary technology. Keep moving forward, or you will get caught in the trap and be converted into a lost soul. It takes time and wisdom to read a person properly. The red flags never lie. Listen carefully to others as they reveal themselves to you, and believe the dark things they tell about themselves. When a double agent has been identified, you must fall back. You are not here to rescue the other players from their twisted self-destructive behaviors. The game waits for no one. Only those who persevere will accomplish their goals.

The unknowing player wanders through the game interacting with various players and pawns. The wise player understands the principles and carefully chooses alliances. The energy and mindset we carry with us draw similar energy to us. To succeed on this level stay in touch with your thoughts, goals, emotions, and frequency at all times. If you are pulling in distractors, it is a glimpse into your scattered unconscious mind. I challenge you to question what you have been conditioned to believe. Are you ready to strive for more? Do you believe you deserve better in this life? As well, assess how successful such beliefs have been for those who instilled them in you. You may be surprised at what you find. Reclaim your power in this pursuit by utilizing what is working and re-working what is not productive. Level yourself up to attain the alliances you wish. It begins with you.

Every principle in this guidebook is meant to optimize your success. Relationships can be a life building focused energy booster or a quagmire of destruction. Most relationships exist somewhere in-between. Take note of those that may still be holding you back from your highest self. There are to be no limits on whose destructive tendencies you choose to remove from your game; NO

ONE is off-limits. Assess relationships wisely. Are your relationships abusive, controlling, narcissistic, neglectful, or are your loved ones unwilling to address the issues? Unconditional love with the exception of underage children due to the nature of the caregiver/dependent relationship is a fallacy. There can come a point which you get sucked into the never-ending chaos as well. You will know when it is time to let go and move on to a better life. Aligning with the correct people in both your professional and personal life can lead to lasting love in friendships and relationships, but love and relationships of all kinds come with conditions.

The following *Principles for Successful Alliances* are an exercise on questioning your current belief system and the relationships you have allowed in your life. Who are you allowing to hold you back from accomplishing the most of your life? And, what alliances have you made that are helping you win the missions and make your life better for generations to come? Mastery comes from balancing every facet of the game.

- *Principles for Successful Alliances* -

Principle 1: Mutual Benefits Must Be Retained

In every alliance, familial relationship, friendship, business relationship, as well as romantic relationships, there must exist equality in admiration, workload distribution, and overall benefits. When a balance is lacking resentments and anger build, and eventually the relationship deteriorates. At that point, the worst traits are brought out in both players resulting in a downward spiral of the ego. Do not let other's critiques of you destroy your self-worth. Is another player in the game weighing you down? Are you carrying the entire team? It may be time to renegotiate the relationship, or it could be time to progress alone on your journey. Dead weight will only slow you down.

There are players in this game who will fail. There are those who have been so damaged by the game that they have already been defeated. Only the strong-minded and emotionally intelligent will rebound from the challenges they face to succeed. You cannot make another player want to win, nor can you play their game for them. Be kind, be honestly forthright, and hold fast to your boundaries. A change will occur when the difficulties outweigh the benefits; you will know when that time comes. You must recognize your purpose and move forward, with or without them.

It is important to know that new players will enter your circle at the proper time as you level-up in the game. Our world is more abundant than you have been led to believe. Your persistent personal growth will automatically place the right people into your life; like attracts like. Work diligently to keep your mental state in the present moment. The past was a lesson to project you further into the game.

Although there will never exist a perfect balance within a relationship of any kind, it is important to communicate openly with all parties involved if relationships are to be retained. A pivotal mistake made by many is withholding feelings and thoughts on a matter to spare the other party's feelings. However, this is the exact point at which issues should be addressed, prior to allowing them to fester and create destructive emotion. There is a higher principle that we must work toward to remain in relationships. Typically, our primitive brain is triggered and causes a desire to leave. Do you recognize these triggers in your own life?

It is so often that we leave relationships, only to re-seek the same conditions to continue the unaddressed cycle. Our minds have a way of creating stories about situations that may not be accurate. Ask questions, clarify, and remain open. It is time to rethink the status quo and create communication that retains mutual benefits for all players. What have you been holding back that needs to be addressed? How are your relationships off balance, and how would you like to see them repaired? Whether you know it or not, your fear of direct communication is probably impacting your relationships for the worse.

Principle 2: All Players Must Retain Their Individuality

An alliance brings people together; however, each player must remain an individual with their own experiences, goals, and destiny. When boundaries become blurred, the players take on a controlling nature and sense of entitlement over the other players. Free will must remain intact. Have you retained your individuality within your relationships, or have the lines become muddy between you and those around you? Do you have your own interests, goals, desires, and purpose outside of your relationships?

Each soul placed in this realm was brought here as an individual and must fundamentally remain that way until it returns to the Source at the completion of the game. Alliances are of great importance and necessary, however, the game is an individual experience with community players working together toward common goals. If you intermingle your player too much with others and project your expectations on them, they cannot be free to play up to their potential and neither can you. Furthermore, this creates a distraction from both party's objectives, and then subsequently, misdirection. Retain your personal power while working interdependently with others. You must remain true to your game, as well as allow others to play theirs.

The most common example of intermingling of these boundaries I have observed and experienced on my journey is with families. Due to the nature of the family bond it is understandable why this occurs most often. However, it can be destructive. Husbands and wives can lose their independence once the marriage occurs, especially with the onset of parenthood. Insecurity, lack of self, undefined purpose can lead to over attachment. It is important to balance the need for parent-child time with husband-wife time, as well as allow time outside of the family for all members involved. The family is an amazing dynamic, but all relationships experience growth and change so there must be time allotted for such growth.

How are you facilitating individuality within your relationships? Have you lost yourself to your role within the relationship? What steps are you going to take to reclaim your singularity while still fulfilling your roles within your relationships? New ideas and growth occur in these times of solace. Allow for these moments of self-discovery and progression on your quest.

Principle 3: A Mutual Goal Must Exist Between the Players

When an alliance is formed, sometimes regardless of function, the underlying energy that binds the players is the mutual goal. Often these bonds are developed to meet a specific cyclic need, and when that need has been achieved, the relationship eventually dissipates. A long-term bond must be created with caution. The alliance is to be chosen wisely. If both players continue to grow individually as well as within the relationship by recreating healthy bonds utilizing the *Principles*, it will thrust both players forward on their missions. If not, they can become un-energized and stagnant within the game.

Be mindful that growth happens in spurts. When you are young and enter school, you are energized, but very few people can retain that momentum until graduation. The same can occur with a career or a romantic relationship. When the game is new it is exciting; active learning takes place. What is the binding force in your relationships? Can you identify a mutual goal either expressed or implied between yourself and others in your circle?

Players for various reasons create bonds; traumas bind some for spiritual healing, families are created for obvious reasons, friendships based on commonality, and employment for practical and growth potential. After the lessons have been learned and growth slows or ceases to happen a person's energy becomes diminished. If not careful, the goals can no longer be identified, or they may have been completed with no subsequent goals in place. Commonly, society has been programmed to search for meaningless distractions when this occurs.

Have you come to a point at which you are coasting through life instead of living it? Have distractions taken over your life? Are your alliances lacking inspiration and unable to identify their goals? Beware when players in the game cannot identify purpose, motivation, goals, and core beliefs that are meant to propel them to the end of the game. When this occurs, they begin to make poor choices with their time, and their lives become out of balance.

Televisions, computers, video games, sports, rolling the dice, shopping, unsafe sex, alcohol, overeating, and drug use, are these binding you to other players? These are the societal distractors, which have been implemented by others seeking their victories in the game. As they become more and more socially acceptable forms of distraction, you must become even stronger to avoid their grip. Do you feel stuck around people who cannot see past these vices and distractors? When others around you have chosen a lowered state of existence as their norm, it is time to level-up your own game. A winning player distances themselves from all habit-forming distractions, which provide no direct benefit to their purpose within the game.

One hopeful yet mysterious endeavor that many enter into is marriage. In our society it is quite a taboo topic in which families typically refrain from discussing the intricate details, or the ongoing goals of the union. Instead, they highlight the superficialities of the relationship. Seemingly, the husband-wife dynamic would work similarly to any other relationship in the fact that the two parties would certainly have their disagreements, but would continue to work toward the mutual goals and a common understanding. The goal: to retain the relationship as well as a flourishing familial group. How has your history shaped your perception of the family union? What ideals have you changed within your own familial group? What has remained the same?

In my family, I never witnessed my parents arguing or even disagreeing. Then, when I reached second grade my parents sat my sister and me down to announce their impending divorce. I experienced great confusion within myself when this happened, and I can even later recall thinking that the lacks of confrontation or disagreement were healthy ways to handle a marriage. I carried this unhealthy cycle into my own marriages and prided myself on lack of conflict within my relationships. That however, did not mean that they were free from challenges, only that the challenges did not get addressed or resolved. The cycle continued. Destructive and meaningless distractions were instead injected into the family in many forms.

How many marriages can you think of that are fraught with affairs, physical and substance abuse, lack of intimacy, or spouses who are mentally checked out? How many children are being raised by television, video games, or by their smart phones and tablets? Parents are unconsciously allowing themselves to become over stressed and overworked, and so are their children because the players are living out of sync with the game. Within two generations the family unit has been badly damaged. Broken families are becoming the new norm, and for those who strive for strong family bonds it has become increasingly difficult to find a proper mentor to guide them. The choice to participate in such unhealthy states is up to the players, but poor choices come with serious consequences.

Children who have not been shown proper examples will continue the cycle without adequate intervention and practical demonstration. It is time to rebuild the base goals and purpose for our existence, the family, and strive for our individual purposes as well. The cycle has to be identified and a plan in place to reach the desired result. In your own life, you must make the choice to stop the cycles of destruction to win the game.

You must be aware of these patterns and avoid the mistakes of the ordinary player. If your current game cannot keep your attention without resorting to self-destructive distractions (smoking, drugs, rolling the dice, shopping, alcohol, overeating, high risk sex, technology over-use, sedentary behaviors) and alliances that support those decisions, it is time to make a change. Mutually set goals within alliances, create action plans, and set forth to win in your relationships. What is bringing you purpose at this moment? The more you align with your real mission the distractions will fade away into the background.

This is a game of self-reflection and reassessment. Where are you in the game and where you are headed? What is your plan to get back on track? Fear of the game keeps many from living to their fullest potential, but not you. You are here to win. Push forward when fear enters your consciousness. All things are possible within you; your mind creates your reality.

Building and Achieving Goals: Tools for Your Arsenal

1.   What is my goal? (Example: obtain a promotion at work)

Understand your individual strengths, which no one else possesses. You are competing with others on a certain level, but you cannot try to emulate someone else's innate abilities. Instead, focus on your own natural talents and how those set you apart from your competition. You can have the same basic skill set as others, but you need to stand out in an individual way that highlights what you can bring to the table for the company to grow.

- Are you a mathematical genius?
- Are you a leader when it comes to customer relations?
- Are you a master marketer?
- Is the psychology of handling difficult situations your forte'?

In my position, my fellow team members have similar skills, but we also have highly individualized skills like those listed above, which help us take it to the next level. Always play off of your own skills in an interview.

2.   What pieces am I missing to achieve the goal?

- Specific skill sets?
- Marketing knowhow?
- Guest retention strategies?
- Guest dispute resolution?
- Employee relation skills, etc.?

3.   **How am I going to acquire the information that will help me achieve my goal?**

- Books
- Seminars
- Classes
- Higher Education
- Mentors
- Coaches

4.   **What have I learned? (Write an interview outline)**

- What do you want to be known about you? (History of your successes.)
- What have you done RECENTLY to obtain your goal? (Show them your hunger.)
- Combat your weaknesses by thinking of something that was a weakness in the past, but because you read _____ book, or attended _____ seminar, or when _____ mentored you, you learned X, Y, and Z. Let them know that your weakness is something you have been addressing.
- IMPORTANT: Read the *interview outline* aloud 3-5 times a day for a week until you sufficiently take in the material and align with the talking points.

5.   **Apply the Knowledge (The interview process)**

- Remember that an interview is just a friendly conversation. You want to feel and be comfortable during the interview, which is why the *interview outline* MUST be read through several times daily in preparation.
- Thank the interviewers for the opportunity. Be excited.

- Answer the interview questions in a way that gets all of your talking points into the conversations. You NEED them to know these things about you!
- Answer the questions in a manner that explains...what you are going to do for them (the company), and how you are going to make their business more successful. Remember it is always about the business!
- Express gratitude for everyone who has supported you, believed in you, given you a chance, and mentored you in the past to get you to this position. Be grateful.
- Ask a question. You want to see if the company is a fit for your vision as well.
  1. What are some of the departmental goals for the up-coming year?
  2. I see you have a new marketing strategy. What direction is the company headed?
  3. What are some ways that the company is looking to _____ in the future? Make your questions based on your strengths, so that you can highlight again how you can help the company achieve their goals.
- Thank the interviewers for the opportunity and let them know you look forward to hearing from them about the position.

Write Your Goal

(Personal, Financial, Health, Relationship, etc.)

1.   **What is my goal?**

   - _____

2.   **What pieces am I missing to achieve the goal?**

   - _____

   - _____

   - _____

3.   **How am I going to acquire the information that will help me achieve my goal?**

   - _____

   - _____

   - _____

   - _____

4.   **What have I learned? (Assess Your Growth)**

- _____

- _____

- _____

5.   **Apply The Knowledge (Check for a Win)**

- _____

- _____

- _____

Principle 4: All Players Must Understand Their Role Within the Alliance

Each alliance you enter into naturally occurs with a predetermined role. You are playing a character to meet the shared objectives with other players. The functions of each player must be clearly communicated and well-defined to work with each other and accomplish the tasks at hand. What roles have you taken on to win the game? Are your goals in alignment with your roles?

On a basic level, teacher-student, parent-child, husband-wife, supervisor-subordinate, and mutual friendships each character plays a critical function in our lives. Broken down further, each player has a need to understand the specific tasks necessary to complete the mission successfully. Are you playing a support role? Are you the leader? Is nurturing your role? Do you find yourself being the listener in your role? Are you an advisor? To be most effective in your collaboration the ego must remain in check, or it can deteriorate the alliance. Each role is to be respected mutually.

In a functional alliance, each player moves freely and in unison with his or her counterpart. In a working relationship, a breakdown occurs when the chain of command is disrupted. Other failures can happen when a subordinate attempts to insert their opinion without first understanding the decisions coming from the group leaders. There is an order for successful operations that must be upheld to accomplish the goals of any relationship. Remember your role. If you want to interject your thoughts on another level, you must first reach that level to not only have your opinions respected, but to have a grasp of the unknown agendas coming down from above. The inmates cannot run the asylum, nor can you effectively work outside of your role in the game. Recognize that doing so without being encouraged to creates friction within the alliance. Instead, be in a position that your interjections are a necessity toward forward progress. Live in your most effective role. Are you stepping outside of your role in your relationships? If so, it may be time to level-up.

Within a traditional family dynamic, the woman plays one role and the husband another. Because of the increase in divorce and single-parent households the roles have been muddled. Parents feel pressure to take on a two-parent role, but this is not feasible. A parent can and should only take on their role. A mother cannot be a father, nor can a father be a mother. The woman's most effective role is divinely feminine, and a male's most effective role is divinely masculine. A woman's power is in the femininity, but in this modern day, the trend is to try and make up for the lack of opposing energy within the household. Instead, it is advised to allow the opposing energy to come from outside of the familial group. Understand your role and the power innately inside of yourself.

Principle 5: Understand That Unchallenged Traumas from the Past Will Create Destructive Behavior Patterns Within the Alliance, If Not Addressed

The advanced player plays the game for an understanding of him or herself. What makes me tick? Why do I respond in the manner that I do? Why am I being triggered? We must realize that we are energy and that energy from the past can be disruptive to our current agenda.

In the beginning, we came into this world innocent as the Creator intended. Throughout our journey, our pure bodies, minds, and spirits have been corrupted by outside programming. It is imperative when deciding to win on this journey that you understand your individual programming. What memories stand out from your childhood? What triggers dark emotion in your life? Do you continue to be in relationships with the same kinds of people only to experience the same dire results? What self-destructive behaviors do you have? How are your relationships with family members? Do you remain in a job where you find no fulfillment or growth? Question every aspect of your life that is not working for you. That is where your belief system is off and self-challenges remain. Recognizing the disconnect in your thoughts allows you the opportunity to adopt a new belief system, recover, and move forward to complete your objectives.

Abuse of any kind, such as neglect, physical, narcissistic, or sexual abuse and your resulting habitual responses of self-talk, destructive behavior, and harmful alliances, can ripple on through your life and destroy your journey until you recognize and change your cycles. Acknowledge both the positive and negative traits that someone has brought into your life. Duality exists in this world; do not be one-sided in your views. It is time to take a look deep inside to see what has interrupted the success of your game.

As a divorced woman who has come to recognize familial patterns, I could tell that some of my patterns began prior to my birth. As I wrote previously, my mother's natural father abandoned my mother, her siblings, and my grandmother when my mother was a child. Although she was fortunate to have a fantastic stepfather, my mother still unconsciously held onto her abandonment issues.

This abandonment issue led to an unconscious yearning and search for male affirmation. My mother then married my father who also could not be present in the way that she needed. The pattern resumed, the pain was felt all over again, and a sense of unworthiness and hopelessness planted itself even deeper into the psyche. This pattern was all that my mother had known in her life. It was a familial pattern. Her father was not there for her emotionally, and without conscious awareness, she was trying to heal that emotional wound with my father and several relationships afterward. Due to the deficiency caused by the abandonment in my mother, I was either genetically imprinted with or nurtured to include the same deficiency.

Fast-forward, I watched this pattern throughout my childhood, and although I thought of my childhood as quite normal, I picked up the same belief system. I had been in two marriages before I recognized the same pattern of bringing people into my life that could not emotionally connect in the way I needed, nor could they support my life's purpose, so an abandonment of sorts eventually occurred. Because of the deficiency, I made unconscious choices to bring people into my life that would allow me to feel the cycle over and over, with the unconscious hope of healing the wound. It was time to recognize and stop the cycle, and attract the right alliances in my life with purposeful action to remain true to myself and my purpose, boundaries, and core beliefs.

We must look at whom we attract into our lives and take responsibility for where we are today. It is not the other person's fault. Most of them are not bad people. They are just the wrong alliances for your purpose. You are attracting them into your life, which is wreaking unproductive havoc on your journey. What patterns have been carried through your family; divorce, abandonment, addiction, physical or sexual abuse, financial devastation, food addiction, poor health?

Are you ready to do the work to take your life in a new direction? The first step is to acknowledge; the second is to take action. Understand yourself and let go of what is no longer serving you on your journey; if you want to win you have to be around the winners. Define your goals. It is time to step outside of your comfort zone, level-up in the game, and move toward people who always seemed out of reach.

To accomplish this feat you must first fundamentally understand that we are all human beings, therefore, all on the same playing field. We are all born with potential. Although, some are born with more opportunity readily available to them, we are all able to strive for more that we currently have. This wantingness is the mind-set that will allow you to step out of your comfort zone and reach for more. Opportunity is available for those who strive to obtain it. Identify what traits you want to embody and take the necessary steps to become those qualities. Courage is a muscle, which must be exercised. History is fraught with examples of the under-dog who overcame. Continually immerse yourself in these teachings for inspiration.

Act like the winner you were meant to be, raise your standards within yourself, and walk away from those and those who do not complement your purpose. When you act like a winner, the Universe will send more winners your way. Your attention will be drawn to those like-minded individuals. Finally, align yourself with players who want to progress in the game, and not those who wish to remain victims of it.

Challenge Your Past

➢ **What triggers undesirable emotions in your life?**

- _____

- _____

- _____

➢ **When have you felt this way in the past?**

- _____

- _____

- _____

➢ **Identify family cycles you have allowed into your life.**

- _____

- _____

- _____

➢ **What traumas are still affecting your journey?**

- _____

- _____

- _____

Chapter 5

Increase Your Health

If someone wishes for good health, one must first ask oneself if he is ready to do away with the reasons for his illness. Only then is it possible to help him.

- Hippocrates

Since the time when man understood sacred knowledge, the hidden influential powers also began to infiltrate the minds of society. Under the guise of societal, religious, and political leaders as well as teachers and healers, the world underwent a dramatic change. Those human beings that were unaware of the agenda increasingly became diminished spirit power sources. They began wandering through existence lost and unaware of the powerful beings they once were.

What once was a paradise world of enlightened gods had been degraded nearly out of existence through genetic weakening and lack of sacred internal knowledge. The birthright was taken from the players and placed outside of their beings as external gods whom power must be surrendered too. Divine power had become an image of an unattainable ideal, instead of a reflection of inner wisdom and beliefs.

The changes had occurred so slowly over the millennia that man had become desensitized to these devastating changes. Are you prepared to regain your inner knowledge and repair yourself for the remainder of your journey? Your objective is to reacquire the remaining ancient understanding possessed by the shaman, tribesman, medicine men, and herbalists - much of which has been repressed or represented as myth. They hold the key that will allow human beings the innate power to heal themselves.

These groups of divine healers understood that given the proper point of homeostasis the cells begin to regenerate and energy could flow freely throughout the body. Once the players stopped the destructive cycles taught to them by the modern world and returned to the sacred knowledge, the mind would reclaim its calmness, and inspirational ideas would enter from a long forgotten plane of consciousness. Be careful who you place your precious health in the hands of; health is very simple and should remain that way.

In the game, very few similarities among human beings have remained in common with the original players. The gods were led to believe that allopathic medicine was the new God and human beings were helpless spectators in their own lives. The original players were placed around the equator with abundant sunshine, fresh fruits, moderate temperatures, and clean water. At some point preceding the fall of humans, the world became co-inhabited by beings that fed off of a manufactured darker energy, much different than the light energy eaten by the gods. The people's internal energy centers became off center, and so did the Earth. It remains that way today.

Life as it was known began to change; famine occurred, people fled paradise and moved toward the cooler northern climates, and diets were altered as a result. Humans became clouded in the body, thoughts, and judgment. The energy that once flowed freely through their bodies became stuck and disease formed within these blocked energy fields. The once abundant sunshine was now covered with clouds and gray skies. After only a few generations, people completely forgot that they were once gods and now identified as being mortal men.

The game had changed. Greed and anger became commonplace. Nature became a commodity. The persuaders flourished by learning how to move several steps ahead of the common man. They were once undetectable players and now able to openly exploit the game even further.

To win the game at this level, which is highly linked with the *Principle* of *One Life, One Avatar,* you must regain your health and longevity. Beware of the social programming, propaganda, and confusion techniques that have been employed against you since day one of the game. Perfection toward the ideal is unattainable. It is not what you accomplish some of the time that matters; it is what you achieve most of the time that helps you win the game. Observe for yourself and learn to fine-tune your actions and instincts, which will move you in the right direction.

With the increase in disinformation and social indoctrination, health has been taken out of the hands of the people and placed with exclusive players. It is commonplace for people to be placed in a cycle of 'care' in which their money is depleted while their health remains in decline until they are so weak that they eventually die, with broken bodies and spirits. Does it make one wonder, just who is benefitting from this diversionary tactic?

At what point did man become wiser that the Creator of this world? It is time to reclaim your birthright of health, clarity of mind and longevity. The principles are simple and the benefits exponential. Take heed that the further you are along the allopathic path, the more challenging your recovery may be. Again, it is up to you. Your life and your health are well within your control.

Principle 1: Winning Lessons from the Past

On your quest, you will come across a food system that has been revolutionized dramatically within the last century. Family farms have been taken over by agricultural giants and factory farming. Pesticides, herbicides, GMO (Genetically Modified Organisms) crops, and synthetic fertilizers are the new norm. Man is becoming increasingly out of sync with nature. Human beings are being sucked into a dangerous game that has been in the works for generations. We have been slowly limited with our food choices and falsely led to believe that progress is being made.

Gardens have taken a back seat, and an increasing number of Home Owner's Associations deter people from planting food-bearing plants in order to 'sustain' neighborhood values and keep wildlife at bay. A significant distractor within the system we live in is the idea that our current meat supply is a safe consumable source of protein. Perhaps it was long ago, but currently, due to the manner in which these animals have been raised, they are experiencing the same energy blocks and disease that human beings now encounter. The animals are not only raised outside of their natural habitat, but they are deprived of life-sustaining sunshine, familial groups, exercise, and fed a diet out of sync with their natural way of life. The stresses that they experience living in such conditions have been retained within their bodies and are consumed by the humans who eat their flesh.

Ingesting this less than ideal vital force energy, known as 'chi' by the Chinese, or 'e-yon-yee' by the Pueblo Indians, produces energetic deficiencies within our bodies as well. To restore optimal energy flow throughout the earthly body, one must either avoid eating animal products that have been raised out of sync with nature or choose options grown as closely aligned with nature as possible.

How many people are aware of the conditions in which their food is being raised? Many years ago, I was a chaperone during an elementary school field trip to a mid-sized dairy farm in Arizona. It was an awakening experience to see first-hand the crowded conditions in which the cattle lived. The herd would stand day by day, hour after hour, in several inches of their feces, all while eating GMO corn and drinking stagnant water. They would spend their entire lives in these conditions. There would be no reprieve from their waste. These fecal and urinary acids would leach up through their hooves into their meat and milk supplies, just as the chemicals from artificial acrylic nails and nail polish leach through the nail beds of unsuspecting woman everywhere. Such compounds can be detected in human breast milk. After our visit to the farm, I could then identify the taste of cow waste in any conventional meat I consumed from that day forward. I began to understand the smoke and mirrors presented to us as consumers. The television commercials with happy cows, the children's farm coloring books, and the picturesque green pasture are highly misleading to the consumer. So, how does naturally raised meat and dairy actually taste?

Was this what our ancestors remembered food tasting like? My own great-grandparents were farmers. They lived a simple life and I was grateful to have known my great grandmother and her ways of life. Over the years I would recall a story my mother had retold since I was a young girl growing up in Hillsdale, Michigan. My great grandmother was born in 1894, prior to the pasteurization of milk. Her family enjoyed dairy in the freshest way, straight from the cow. Once they began pasteurizing milk, my great grandmother stopped drinking it. She would proclaim, "that isn't milk," and she was correct in the sense that the structure of milk and all foods change through the process of cooking. Fruits, vegetables, meats, and dairy, along with every living thing in our world contain this 'chi' or 'e-yon-yee,' which becomes diminished when heated above 118 degrees Fahrenheit.

It is possible within the next generation that people will not remember that cows used to graze on grass in open fields, but instead eat GMO corn through metal-grated troughs. People will not know milk prior to antibiotics just as they do not recall it in its natural raw state, nor will they remember moderation in meat consumption. We have been programmed to over-consume and trust the experts. To win in the game, however, we must remember where we came from and question why those changes came about.

Principle 2: Eating for the Win

As the hero in your own game, it is time to raise your awareness within this system and look out for your own success. You must balance your health goals equally with your *Quest for Riches* as well as *Choosing Alliances Wisely*, so that you may uphold your physical life and your spiritual journey. All must work in harmony. The more you balance and accomplish the objectives outlined for you, the further along you will progress on your quest. Health is pivotal to winning your game.

You have been led to believe that food-like products are nourishing to the body. Pre-packaged foods have replaced home cooking and family meals are becoming a thing of the past. Players with different aims are hijacking the human connection to food growth, preparation, and enjoyment. Preservatives, additives, synthetically colored foods, and product mascots are being marketed to the unsuspecting masses in an attempt to imprison their wealth, health, and their minds for further consumerism and energy harvesting. It has only taken a few generations to change the concept of food; it is time to wake up and return to godlike food sources.

For some time, after my experience on the farm and remembering back to visits on my three uncles' conventional hog farm, I chose to switch our family over to grass-fed organic meat, and later to turkey burger until we finally gave up meat altogether. To make the transition easier for a family who had been raised on the standard American diet, we started purchasing 'meat alternatives' like veggie burgers, 'chicken' strips, meatless meatballs, and many more.

After transitioning to meat alternatives, we made another transition to a more whole plant-based lifestyle with a focus on fresh raw fruits and vegetables. We limited cereal by eating fruits in the morning, we limited nearly all canned foods unless they were in glass containers, and we switched to no-sugar-added vanilla almond milk or original almond milk depending on the recipe.

We taught ourselves how to critique food labels to see past the marketing and understand what we chose to purchase. We learned how to make sauces, create salads with and without lettuce; we snacked on fresh guacamole and salsa. Avocado became our cheese. Cucumbers became our chips, and zucchini and squash became our noodles. Fresh and frozen grapes, strawberries, blackberries, blueberries, melons, and fruit smoothies became our snacks.

We had fun with our new lifestyle by making veggie sushi rolls and veggie spring rolls with fresh herbs, we read recipes and watched videos to capture more ideas. East Indian curries satisfied our savory needs, everyone in the household enjoyed the Asian stir-frys we prepared, and Mexican foods were easily converted using fresh plant-based options.

Winners take the time to figure out how to win; we loved a challenge. During the summer we juiced at least one watermelon everyday and during the winter we switched to juicing 60 pounds of fresh local oranges every week. It took some time and creativity, but we had abundant choices in our lives and experienced an equal amount of health benefits from moving away from animal products.

Changing our food choices changed not only our taste buds, but also the dynamics of food preparation within our household. Everyone picked out their favorite fresh food at the store and everyone helped wash, cut, and prepare our meals. Our once picky eaters were now much more healthy-minded eaters. We sleep better, we were calmer, we were closer, and we had each experienced our own individual health benefits.

To be the most optimal hero in the game, it is advised to forgo all highly processed and animal products. Humans have been diminished with additives, dyes, chemicals, and other non-food products for nearly a century. Health has been in steady decline; fertility continues to decline, cancer rates are soaring, Autism is on the rise, autoimmune and inflammatory disease remains rampant, and stress and anxiety are out of control. Allopathic medicine remains ignorant of the causes, and the pharmaceutical makers continue to get rich in the process.

Taking back ownership of your health is a powerful move in this game. It puts you back in the driver's seat of your health and finances. As you move toward a plant-based diet, your body will slowly begin to heal. Begin by increasing your fruit intake. Fruit is one of the purest filtered water sources on the plant. Its electrical qualities will wake your body in the morning and keep it steady throughout the day. Your mood will lift, your skin will glow and become softened, and your eyes will become brighter.

In my own experience, I had gone through a decline in my vision before becoming a plant-based eater, but through intermittent fasting on fruit juice, herbs and high raw food intake my vision improved. I no longer need prescription glasses. When I steered away from bread products my dry skin improved, and when I went vegan my joints stopped hurting. My body experienced a dramatic improvement in overall inflammation and allergies of all kinds disappeared.

Humans do not even realize how sick they actually are. Most have lost their physical energy and childlike playfulness. When was the last time you played like a child, ran in nature, climbed a tree, played tag, or hide and seek? The players forget that they were once gods, living in harmony with the laws of nature. Many have rolled over and accepted poor health in the name of aging. It is time to reclaim your throne and your power. Throw away what does not serve you, plan your meals to plan your health, forgo the three-meal a day and food pyramid recommendations that has led to our decline. There will always be a new tagline: low-fat, high fiber, high protein, cholesterol free. You do not need the confused sciences to tell you how to fuel your body. When you get back to a natural diet, there will be no taglines.

Your primary objective is to shop in the produce section, read labels to avoid complicated ingredients lists, and re-teach yourself the basics. Eat fresh. If your ancestors would not recognize it as food, then leave it alone. It really is that simple. You reap what you sow, you are what you eat, and it is up to you to make it happen. Are you ready to increase your energy, health, and vitality and get back in the game?

Also imperative is avoiding alliances that do not allow you to be successful in your quest for health. Many will fail on this journey. Will power will only get you so far. It is important to set yourself up for a win by placing yourself around those with similar goals for the win. Set your sights on the finish line. Your new alliances will be waiting to take you the rest of the way.

- ➢ **Challenge: Go through your pantry and refrigerator, read the labels on your food items, sort, and donate all food items that are not in alignment with your current mission. Research new recipes that will get you excited about your new journey.**
- ➢ **Note: Alternative plant-based recipes are available for nearly all of your current favorite recipes. The key is using fresh herbs for flavoring.**

Principle 3: Connecting with Your Natural Power

When human beings first inhabited this world, they fully understood the innate powers given to them by the Source. They were connected to the eternal power and lived as one with the infinite planet, natural laws, as well as each other. Following the fall of mankind, industrialization, and the modernization of society, humans have been heavily influenced into consumerism, indebtedness, and the lack of introspection of their actions. Outside forces have interjected their own desire to win at the expense of our unsuspecting people.

Your training began the moment you entered school, perhaps even prior. Taught a fractional historical view of the world and science, you have been trained to be a pawn worker within the game. You were synthesized to enter the game with a preprogrammed mindset to work for the betterment of the elite, noble and royal players in this game. They give you the options they see fit and shape your perception of yourself and your world. *Change your thoughts to change your reality.* Your mind has been transformed into an invisible enemy. During this challenge, you will reconnect with your natural self.

With the improvement of your diet as well as the lessening of the chemical intake within your body you will experience an increase in your natural intuition. However, that is just the first step. The second is to reconnect with nature. How often do you physically connect with the living Earth? We are electrical beings who must connect physically with the equally electrical planet. How were the original people connected with nature?

The first people in Paradise either lived in primitive structures on the ground with earth floors or perhaps in raised housing in cliff dwellings or among the trees, which kept them close to the natural elements. They picked and ate fruit among the trees, ate greens and herbs low to the ground, and eventually hunted and fished. Every day began with the rising sun and ended when the world fell into darkness. Their lives were filled with rituals, which brought them closer to their divine selves. They took notice of the constellations, the sun and moon, seasons and changes in the weather, and rain patterns. The earliest people were forced to be in tune with the natural laws.

As a technologically advanced society it is not likely for us to return to such ways of living, nor would many of us wish too. However, we can take lessons from the ways in which our ancestors lived and won in this realm. We must understand that many changes that have come about by the ideas of man are making us ill and out of balance. Belief systems have become confused based on the numerous conflicting news media stories that we have been led to believe. We have been programmed to question our intuition. In this game, it is advised to go back to who you were at the beginning of the game; before the programming began.

Why would we cover our eyes with sunglasses, our skin with sunscreen, and our bodies with chemical sprays? Is it believable that that which created us as a species would allow every other being on this Earth to thrive in their natural bodies except human beings? The sun must serve a purpose for our bodies, or our bodies would have been covered with physical protection. In fact, we eat sunlight in the plants that we consume. We are sunlight, and our bodies benefit, produce hormones, and other processes occur with exposure to the sun's radiance. Our own intuition should lead us to get out of the sun before getting burned by it, rather than coating ourselves with synthetic chemicals which leach into our largest organ, our third kidney, the skin.

As well, the acidic diets of man that causes the illnesses that bring about skin conditions and eye injuries are blamed on our beloved sun. Again, I ask you to consider who benefits from such information? It is those that create the products, as well as those who treat skin disorders, and also those who benefit from the distractions and hysteria the placed attention creates. Yes, some people will experience effects from sun exposure, but that is only a symptom of an underlying imbalance in the way that particular being lives within the natural laws. Once the balance has been restored to the body it will create homeostasis, restoring itself.

The body was born to heal itself. Reconnect with your supreme power and limit the destructive behaviors in your life. Winners get sunshine, enjoy the landscape and plants, breath clean air; eat fresh healing fruits, herbs, soaked seeds and nuts, and vegetables. They rest their bodies and their minds. They understand that undue stress must be removed from their lives, and they make time for physical activity by keeping it simple.

Put your shoes on, or not, and step out into nature, go for a walk, a hike, or a run. Use your body physically to climb, cut, haul, drag, and to lift itself during daily outdoor activities and chores - convenient and practical exercise. Victors have control over their minds and not vice versa. The winners know a strong body and a sharp mind are connected, and that we are connected to our world. We are made from this world and will physically return to it at the end of the game. We are the world and we are the future of it.

Other tips for limiting unnatural exposure in order to get ahead in the game are: turn off the Wi-Fi when going to sleep at night, limit phone, computer and television exposure, unplug unused electronics, do not sleep with your cell phone, keep television out of the bedroom, forgo plastic food storage containers for glass containers, drink and eat off of glass or other natural materials, do not use aluminum in the kitchen, refrain from using synthetically-coated pans in the kitchen, and replace plastic cooking utensils with steel or wooden products.

Also, switch to natural body-care products and omit antiperspirant deodorant products containing aluminum. Wear natural stones and metals in jewelry. Be okay with whom you were made to be by doing away with toxic nail polishes and faux nails.

Accept your naturally changing hair, which shows your age and wisdom; avoid synthetic hair products and implants and injections within the beauty industry. Avoid cutting the body, which changes the lymphatic flow in those areas, making detoxification more challenging.

The more you step back in line with nature the more naturally beautiful you will become. Avoid excessively cutting the hair. Every gift given to man was created to help us win the game. The aging process can reverse to a certain degree and most undoubtedly slow as you hydrate your skin with fresh fruit juices, herbs, and living foods. Your natural light will shine through, and your instincts increase as well as your connection to your loved ones.

Leaders and heroes follow the laws of nature to get ahead. They connect with the planet and the sun for power, spiritual growth, and reconnection to the Source within. They know being in man-made structures and being part of man-made ideals take vital energy from us as humans. Winners limit exposure to things that do not serve their purpose.

> **Challenge: Plan an outdoor activity each day for 14 days (go to the park, take a nature walk, go hiking, pick wild berries, visit an orchard or a vegetable farm, have a picnic, fly a kite, go canoeing or kayaking, take a camping trip, plant an herb garden, rake leaves, or play in the snow).**

Principle 4: Juice Fasting, Detoxification, Herbal Medicine, and Resting the Body

Are your moods unpredictable and easily thrown off? Is your brain foggy? Can't seem to wake up throughout the day? The most profound ways to experience increased health are through the art of detoxification and fasting, the literature on which is endless. For the sake of simplicity and ease, I will outline the most easily accessible ideals, which will help your body quickly recover from the detrimental effects of the modern journey of most players. Detoxification has been extremely downplayed by allopathic medicine and is widely viewed with disdain. However, it has been practiced since man likely inhabited the planet and is spoken about extensively in ancient religious texts. To recover quickly in the game, you must know how to be well, as well as quickly recover from illnesses. Your journey is too remarkable to allow ill health to slow you down.

The animal kingdom's instincts have remained far more intact than nearly every human player in this game. Through observations of nature, how do animals deal with illness? They stop eating, and they rest. Animals place themselves in a self-imposed fasting state to lower the amount of energy they use for digestion, so that the body can use that energy to repair itself. They recognize that the body can go for a very long time without food. In religious texts there have been accounts of fasting for forty days or more, and death was not an outcome of these events. We have become addicted to eating. When we eat, our bodies use massive amounts of energy to digest, especially meat, dairy, and grains.

Take note of how your body feels after a heavy meal of meat, dairy, and grains. Typically, a sedentary activity, gas, bloating and indigestion follow this type of meal. We have been led to believe that we need animal protein for energy, but dead cooked foods will never provide the quickly accessible living energy we get from fruits, herbs, soaked nuts, seeds, and raw vegetables. These foods pass quickly through the digestive system and are eliminated within twelve hours. Most players are constipated to a point that they only eliminate waste one time a day, maybe less. Human beings were made to do so at a much faster rate.

Those elite players have been changing our way of interacting with food systems and limiting our choices in the pursuit of their own abundance in the game, and in addition, creating substandard energy-reducing food guidelines for our people. The grain farmers, the meat growers, and the dairy industry have themselves been manipulated to create a system of energy blocking, illness, and early death. It has been a domino effect since the industrialization of mankind. We have been conditioned to overeat and make improper food combinations. The original humans ate simply, gathering most of their food.

To improve digestion, it is essential to eat the food with the highest water content and lowest density first. Begin with fruits, herbs, followed by raw then cooked vegetables, starches, grains, nuts and meats, that is if you are retaining grains and meats in your diet. Keep it as simple as possible by eating mono-meals or simple combinations of items.

It is advisable to begin the day with fresh fruit juice and continue eating fruits, veggie fruits (cucumbers, tomatoes, peppers, avocados), herbs, and vegetables throughout the day. Eventually, your body will adjust, parasites and yeast will die off, and your body will crave fresh living foods.

If you have come this far in the game by way of the standard American diet, you will benefit significantly from juice fasting. Watermelon is the quickest, readily available and priced inexpensively. Cut the melon in half, score the inside and scoop it into a standard blender with a plunger feature. Blend for approximately ten seconds and enjoy. I recommend one melon a day, two if you have a family. You will experience hydration at levels that water alone can never provide. You will become mentally calm, focused and have constant energy that comes from the living water inside. Fresh living juice is fasting for the modern human being. We have become so toxic from our lifestyles that water fasting alone could be harmful. Only advanced players should water fast with the assistance of a master. Fresh fruit, herb, vegetable juices are sufficient to increase health and detoxify more quickly.

Put you first, health and well-being are key components of this game. Once you get your finances in order, the cost of your well-care will be offset by your decreased cost of allopathic medicine. Medication and frequent doctor visits will become a thing of the past. Prevention will rule your new world. Allopathic medicine is a necessity for emergency care only. By putting these principles in place you are allowing your body the correct environment to fix itself of high blood pressure, diabetes, intestinal distress, inflammation, skin issues, and more. You will learn that symptoms are signs that energy blocks still exist and that you need to dig deeper into your healing process.

I recall my first visit to a general practitioner as a young woman striking out on my own, and sitting in the waiting room pre-appointment I was asked to fill out a Family Medical History questionnaire. The form asked me to review the diseases and conditions and indicate whom in the family it inflicted, including maternal and paternal relations. As I read down the list, I came across arthritis, high blood pressure, and heart disease, all of which I identified with my paternal grandfather who drove a semi-truck, ate fast food, was a former alcoholic, smoked cigarettes, and lived a sedentary existence. When my grandfather would return home from his cross-country trips, he would sit in his lounge chair watching television, only getting up to eat. Something inside of me could not and would not identify those conditions with my future reality. My life would be different, and I chose to be free from those thoughts that day. I did not place a checkmark next to any disease or condition presented on that paper no matter whom in my family had suffered from it. I would create my own reality within the game.

We are not bound to diseases or life expectancy strictly because of heredity lineage. Our thoughts and beliefs shape our reality. Be careful what you allow to shape your mind. Do not put emotions of fear behind such ideas. When I continued to read, I came across stomach cancer, which afflicted my paternal grandmother. Although she did not live the same lifestyle as my grandfather, she did eat a diet rich in meats, cheeses, and sweets. I also chose not to internalize and align her fate with mine.

I chose to identify my future health based on my beliefs about my maternal great grandmother who had lived a simple life with plenty of fresh air, daily chores, simple foods, small meals, and fresh herbs. My great grandmother lived to be over one hundred years old. She lived alone well into her nineties until she slipped and fell one winter while going down into her cellar. She experienced hypothermia as well as a broken hip that day. Following her fall, she lived with her son's family for many years until she passed away peacefully in her sleep. What health-related ideals have you been identifying within your own life? How you identify with your surroundings changes your future. Play the game carefully and determine your own path. Do not get caught in the path of others as so many do within family structures.

Any player who reaches for over-the-counter medicines or antibiotics and steroids at the first sign of a headache, sore throat, body ache, fever, colds, flu, allergies, intestinal ailment, or skin conditions is not allowing the body the opportunity to alert you to fast or the means to remedy itself. Those methods of warding off minor aches and pains have been fed to us for generations. Keep moving forward with your healing journey, or your illnesses will progress and keep you down in the game, allowing others to win over you. These discomforts are the warning signs to signal you that your body is out of alignment with the natural laws. Ignoring these signs will only push your body further down the rabbit hole to chronic conditions, stress, and dependence on the system.

When this world was created, it was prepared with herbal medicine for the gods. Slowly, these remedies were forgotten and stopped being passed down from generation to generation. All in the name of progress within the medical industry. However, herbalists have retained this ancient knowledge for our future salvation. For every ailment, an herb exists to aid in recovery. With the change in diet, intermittent fasting, and fresh herbs and tinctures the body has all it needs to thrive on your journey. Herbs were meant to level-up your healing. It would serve you well to research herbs that grow locally in your area. There are a number of herbal books available as well as seeds that may be ordered through catalogs for your region. Tinctures are readily available online, or there may be an herbalist in your region. Knowledge is a powerful key in this game. Do your research and move forward in the direction you choose.

Another function of body repair and regeneration is adequate rest for the body. Sleep not only repairs the body but restarts the mind, mood, and allows for dreaming which places us back into the spirit world. Plan your day to allow for adequate sleep. Allow your children the proper sleep that they require, including naps.

Many behavior challenges in children are driven by sleep deprivation, dehydration, hunger, inadequate diets, lack of exercise, fresh air, or sunshine. Listen to your body and listen to the unspoken cues of your children. We must *rest our bodies and rest our minds* to live up to our potential and win this game.

> ➤ **Challenge: Introduce at least one serving of fresh living (unpasteurized) fruit, herb, and/or vegetable juice into your life for the next 30 days.**

Principle 5: The Next Generation of Players

Players of this game should be cautious with whom they share their energy. When sexual alliances occur, universal bonds are created which ripple on throughout time and space. Co-mingling genetic information can also strengthen or weaken the genetic structure of humanity. It is ill-advised to replicate or alter genetics within a laboratory, instead increase health and fertility will follow.

Due to the lifestyle, and current health state of human beings, there will be even higher levels of infertility in the future. Whom may I ask wins at the game when genetic weakening and infertility occurs? It is the same beings that choose to spray our food, and then counteract those detrimental effects by treating us with even more synthetic chemicals in an attempt to heal the degraded body. Be advised that in this game, there are more agendas than the average player can piece together. It is your mission to identify and counteract the operatives.

The controllers in this game seek to infiltrate every aspect of the game; marriage and reproduction have been no exception to this rule. What was once a natural process for a woman has become a medicalized experience for both mother and child. With the advent of fertility drugs, ultra-sounds, genetic testing, blood sugar and other blood testing, urine analysis, C-sections, Pitocin, epidurals, circumcisions, vaccines, and more, it has become a highly profitable business for the practitioner and those forces behind such changes to the industry.

For those experiencing infertility, it is imperative to change diet, introduce moderate outdoor physical activity, and decrease chemical accumulation within the body. Infertility is a sign that the body is out of balance with nature. Realigning with nature will not only increase the chances of fertility, but it will also strengthen the genetics within the mother and father. It is also a necessity to refrain from overuse of electronics. Phones and laptop computers should not be placed on the lap, nor should cell phones stored in pants pockets or near the breasts. Doing so creates electrical interference with the body's natural signals. At every moment you are either strengthening the genetic signals positively within your body or creating a pathway for dis-ease and disharmony.

I have always innately chosen to birth my four children with a midwife with one of the births at a clinic and the others at hospitals. I chose the midwives for their demeanor and my connection to her, and not the location where the birth would take place. My instincts have served me well. I have been outspoken about my wishes and intentions for the births as well as the procedures that I would allow to take place as an experienced birther and person who remained in touch with my body and my limitations.

All of my children were born naturally. The degree of medical intervention between my first two sons and my second two sons decreased. There was neither a need for sugar testing with my last son, nor were there reasons to see the midwife as frequently as customarily recommended, nor did the social conditioning to circumcise and introduce foreign bodies to my babies exist. I began to question all of these practices based on my observations of the world following my dietary changes and increased health as well as a reconnection with my spirituality. My diet and exercise were impeccable with my last two sons, much more than with my first sons. I walked or ran two to four miles every day, I stretched, and I ate naturally and felt great. My moods were calm, I was happy, and my body was strong and ready for the births of my sons.

As a woman, you know your body better than your practitioner. You know if you are gaining or losing too much weight, you know if you are doing too much physically or too little. This is a time of self-awakening and self-awareness. Pregnancy should not be a tiring endeavor. It is not a disease or condition to be treated by the medical profession which is what we are led to believe. It is the most natural divine feminine power a woman will experience in her lifetime.

As a side note, there are indeed circumstances in which allopathic medicine is necessary to intervene in a birth process; I am not speaking about those times. A wise person understands that this guide is meant to assist the player of the game when it comes to reconnecting to themselves and their natural power as a human being. This guide is for those players who wish to advance in the most comprehensive manner possible.

It is essential for you woman players to understand on a spiritual level that your baby will be a projection of the mother during that specific time and point in the mother's journey. The baby feels every emotion, stress, or calmness that the mother feels. It is the most critical time for a mother to be centered and at ease with herself and her pregnancy, so that the baby may come into this world in the same manner. The mother has a responsibility to align only with other players who support her during this time; the pregnancy must not be compromised, no exception.

The father plays a vital role in the mother's emotional and physical well being as the protector and provider of the family. She will look to him during the delivery of the child as support and reassurance that she can accomplish this incredible task. As well, post-pregnancy, the father must be present to emotionally and physically support the mother and baby to create the best environment for the family bond to occur.

Following the birth of your infinite being, your child remains a spirit going between our world and the spirit realm. Refrain from over stimulating the child with unnecessary man-made objects and ideals. Swaddle the child, hold them, let them feel your touch, and help them remain calm during this transition. Nurse the baby skin to skin so that they can feel your energy, warmth, and love. You are creating an eternal bond and creating changes in the universe.

Mothers are increasingly being led to believe that formula is equally as nourishing or even more nourishing than their own breast milk, and that the baby should be weaned within the first year, which should never be assumed. Nature has provided the perfect nourishment for your little one in the form of breast milk. The entire experience is to be decided solely between mother and child.

Nursing should continue until both mother and child decide weaning should take place. If the baby is colicky and spits up the breast milk, the mother's diet needs to be addressed immediately. By switching to a plant-based diet rich in living foods, cutting out grains, dairy, meat and all acidic processed foods the mother's body will become more in line with the natural way of eating. Her energy will increase, her weight will quickly return to pre-pregnancy level, and she will enjoy light activity outdoors very quickly. Use your innate wisdom and instincts to guide your decisions.

If you were nursed when you were an infant, and your mother and grandmother valued nursing, you will likely have a greater sense of confidence and duty to nurse your young. Those women without familial support in the matter will most likely need support from a nursing coach. I had my own challenges when I first began to nurse my oldest son.

I began to waver in my confidence and began to question my ability to continue to nurse. During that time, sister-in-law visited our home. I confided in her my difficulties and wept at my pending failure as a mother. She had breastfed her children, but was reassuring me that not everyone could do it and that maybe I should stop. That was not the response I had hoped to hear. Every single woman in my family had nursed their babies successfully. From her, I had expected to receive the same reassurance that many women struggle, but that it could be done and that it was worth it for the baby. I was so taken back that I dug deep inside of myself and found my own strength to carry on. Things improved, and no matter what difficulties I faced with future nursing I never let it stop me. I reunited with my innate feminine power that day. Persevering through our challenges will help the next generation succeed and overcome their own self-doubt.

When your baby reaches around four months old, you may begin introducing them to real living fruit. To do this, simply purchase a small blending device; you may need to add purified water for the correct consistency. The food must be completely pureed and liquid. Store-bought baby foods should be avoided entirely. They lack living energy due to the pasteurization process, as well as the freshness that your little being requires.

We have been arrogantly led to believe that man can outdo nature and produces superior products, but this is not true. It does not make sense to introduce your baby to foods that your family does not consume on a daily basis. In doing so you are training their taste buds for diminished foods, which will lead them to the self-limiting diets of today's standard American child: chicken nuggets and French fries washed down with an artificially colored drink and a preservative-filled cookie. Instead, as parents, you need to be intentional with your own food choices and raise your child on the real living foods you are eating. Your mission is to set your child up for success within the game from the very beginning.

Continue with fresh fruits and vegetables and when the time comes allow them to be part of the process. Take them to an organic garden where they can pick their own food. Allow them to discover where their food actually comes from. Turn your yard into an edible paradise with your own fruit trees, berry bushes, and vining fruits. Once established your plants will thrive with minimal care and so will your children.

The highest food energy source you can introduce your children to will be the fruits, vegetables, and herbs that you pick on your own property. Ready to eat. We have been conditioned to surround ourselves with ornamental plants, trees and grasses, and then spraying chemicals on them in the name of beauty, instead of creating free and abundant food on our own land. Take ownership of your food choices on your journey to increase your health, vitality, and leave your legacy to those beings you brought into this world.

Principle 6: Leaving the Past Behind

Each day is a blessing and a new beginning. You can only move forward in this game, never backwards. Words, deeds, and actions cannot be undone. Choose all of these things very carefully. To avoid depression stop reliving the past; to prevent anxiety remain in the present moment. Begin each day with a sacred ritual for healing and reconnection with your spirit.

Our brains have compartmentalized our experiences and shaped our personalities to deal with the traumas and events we have experienced. Human beings have become adept at rising and lowering invisible walls to protect us from further trauma. Have you noticed that you unconsciously slip into character roles depending on the situation? There are many facets of our psyche that we do not consciously recognize; therefore we cannot use them to our advantage. We convert to an innocent child when playing with animals, we shift into a leader at work whom our team can count on to make tough decisions, we turn into a protector when our children need security, and we are vulnerable in the face of romance. Our transition is unconscious, but it does not have to be. The more you recognize your emotional triggers from the past, the better you will be able to control your responses. Still feel like a child in front of your parents? Does your authoritative boss make you feel meek? Are you too timid to express your opinions? Are you aggressive while driving or quick to fight? These are signs that your past is impacting your now. Identify, when did you feel this way in the past? And, make a conscious effort to react in a different manner.

The traumas from our lives, the abuse, the neglect, the pain, and all unpleasant experiences will always be a part of our history. You are going to make mistakes in the game, countess, do not let them slow your progress. Do not dwell on their existence. The key in moving forward is to recognize that there are lessons to learn from all of these events. The past will remain unchanged; the future is in your hands. You can choose to be a victim of these events and carry them onto your current reality, or you can understand that not everyone in your future will inflict pain, nor will every future event end with the same dismal results. Learn from your missteps and move ahead in the game.

You were born the purest being imaginable, and unfortunately, people and events have changed the core of who you were meant to be. We are all at degrees of healing, or only just recognizing the impacts of such events. As I said prior, some players check out of the game either mentally or physically because they do not see an escape from the pain. It is critical to go back to your purpose, the reason you have to continue, and be extremely aware of your patterns and things that trigger you. That is where you will find your healing. Resist the urge to linger in your mind, but instead focus on the present. What has been great about today? Is the sun out? Are there breathtaking views outside your door? Is your child joyfully going about his or her day? The little things pull you back into the now. Be grateful.

Beginning the day with calmness gives you the time necessary to get your mind in order and ease into your day instead of rushing from the moment you awaken in the morning. Nourish your body and mind with loving thoughts. For me this is waking one to two hours before the rest of the family, making fresh living watermelon juice and having a cup of herbal tea. I step outside into nature to give myself loving affirmations about the day ahead and blessing the nourishment I am allowing into my body. That includes sitting on the ground among my many fruit trees, bushes, and vines, seated with the warm morning sun on my face, while taking in the sounds of the birds, the breeze and the music of wind chimes. It includes taking notice of the blue sky above and the cloud cover on the most blessed days. Will I be grateful for the ALL that sustains my life and aids in the experience that I came here for? My ritual includes refraining from television, cell phones, and other electronics while centering myself and syncing with the natural laws. What is your daily ritual?

Now is all we have. Are you spending your morning ritual in perpetual stress? Divinity is found in moments of clarity, silence, and nature. When we take the time to get our minds centered, we set ourselves up for a peaceful, purposeful day. A healthy productive ritual does not include rushing to the local coffee shop, rushing to the babysitter or school, or rushing into your job. Everything in a serene morning ritual is allotted with proper time and care. Your family deserves the peace and so does your spirit. The most self-disciplined among the winners are calm in the face of daily life activities. They prepare for their journey, push past their fears, and you must too.

Your clarity and serenity begins the night before. We must allow ourselves adequate sleep for repair of the body and resetting of the mind and emotions. In the evening, we must inventory the day and assess where we want to begin tomorrow. Take care not to dwell on our missteps, but instead move in the direction of your desired results.

Your daily ritual will propel you in the direction of a winning mindset and restoration of the energy focus. From there, it is advisable to introduce affirmations into your daily routine. These reminders can be placed on your electronic device on time intervals to reinforce the direction you are headed in the game. To win, you must believe that you can. From this day forward, you will help yourself along your journey and allow for that win. Each mission is unique; choose your affirmations according to the direction you want your journey to progress.

To make definitive changes to your life takes approximately one month of self-discipline. Your brain will rewire the deeply seated patterns of behavior by forming new neural pathways. Joy will return to your life, and new hopes appear. You will realize your infinite potential in life was shown by your devastating hardships. Life is a series of lessons meant to propel you to your fullest potential. Keep moving forward no matter how difficult the game presents itself. Many players do not make it this far in the game. Fortunately, you are still able to play. Be grateful for every opportunity. You are an infinite being meant for such trying adventures. Perspective teaches us that life was not intended to be free from hardships, but instead full of inevitable trials. The more you allow fear to guide your life, the more difficult it will become.

Take care and begin each new interaction within the game with the innate internal wisdom you have been given.

> ➤ **Challenge: For the next 7 days cut out unnecessary activities (television, computer time, and social media, etc.) and get a full night's sleep. Then, wake up 1 hour earlier to create a relaxing morning routine, which includes a centering morning ritual.**

My Personal Affirmations

- I add VALUE to people's lives

- I attract LOVE

- I attract POSITIVE people

- I am a magnet for ABUNDANCE

- I ARTICULATE my thoughts WELL

- My BOUNDARIES are clear

- My WRITING flows AMPLY

- MY family is LOVING and CLOSE

- I am a SOFT GENTLE woman

- I am CALM and UNDERSTANDING

- I am UNWAIVERING in my CONVICTIONS

- I achieve my GOALS instantaneously

- Energy flows SMOOTHLY through my body

Write Affirmations for Your Journey

- _____

- _____

- _____

- _____

- _____

   Recite your affirmations daily utilizing your electronic calendar on your smart phone. Make your phone work for you by reminding you every hour what you should be thinking throughout the day. Update your affirmations as your goals and needs change.

Chapter 6

Navigating the Map Room

A good plan implemented today is better than a perfect plan implemented tomorrow.

- George Patton

Every game is best played by planning for the win. The more efficient your moves forward and the ease at which you navigate the system, the more quickly you will reach your final destination. The quest of your life is no different. You are playing to win, and the stakes are high. Only your outlook limits the time you have to win, but a strategic plan must be in place.

Our world has been taken over by deadlines and schedules. It is best to prioritize and take care of things as they come. Do not let deeds pile up or go undone. The hidden pressures on your subconscious will weigh you down on your journey. Reactive decision-making is for novice players. Master players take a proactive approach to the game.

The average player wastes several hours during the day. They allow menial tasks to pile-up, they allow clutter into their lives, and their to-do lists never quite get accomplished. Necessary phone calls never get placed, Thank You notes never get written, the book they wanted to read collects dust on the shelf, and they neglect to sign up for the classes they wanted to take. The average player put relationships on autopilot until they crash and burn, and then wonder what went wrong. Their dreams die and eventually so do they with many regrets. Life's wins come first in small victories and in the details, which lead to greater accomplishments and even more victories.

You will become addicted to the victories and identify with the wins. Winning is a great feeling, which helps offset the losses and low points in our lives. As life comes at you, as the ideas hit you, they must be acted upon. Motivation is like a cloud it rolls by and then disappears. You must take action in your life to keep the momentum burning.

Plan the night before for the next morning. Begin your day by reviewing the impending tasks. An organized player gets more accomplished than the haphazard player as they structure their experience. The careless player is distracted by the whims of life, feel that they have no time for anything, and accomplish very little. Avoid those players by raising your stakes. On the other hand, the player with a strategy understands that a specific task best serves each moment. They set out to accomplish the most productive endeavor in each moment while pushing past the fear of failure.

In this world, dream big. Only your internal dialogue limits your success, yet the voice is not your divine voice, but has been hacked by those who have come to shape the world into its own configuration. Remain aware of the presence that is attempting to sabotage your journey. Create your plan, map your path, construct vision boards, write your goals, and/or journal. A well-written goal has a timeline and series of events leading up to as well as surpassing that goal. Begin with the end in mind. What are your gifts, your talents, what creates abundant energy within your body and mind? Your spirit presents your hero-self with the tasks it needs to accomplish on your path. Be receptive and listen to your spirit voice.

Like many, I missed the mark in my life for many years. I did not plan nor did I listen to my spirit trying to communicate my mission with my mind. It took a series of unfortunate events to finally inspire me to act on my purpose. I can remember a moment in junior high school when a friend of mine called me self-righteous when I attempted to set boundaries with her. I shrank myself after that to fit into what she wanted me to be. When I would try to assert myself with others, they would tell me that I was over-thinking, but they did not understand how fundamentally I knew my purpose and myself. The players were attempting to manipulate my game based on their poor understanding of themselves.

As much as sixteen years ago I wrote several children's books and excitedly showed them to a family member. I had inventions come to me numerous times. They were all met with indifference, so I tore them up and went back to being who those without insight into my game wanted me to be. I went back to school to level-up in my life, I read books by influential authors, removed distractions in my life, and listened to people who were winning. But, unfortunately, the people I had accepted into my own life could not recognize my strengths, and I allowed their small minds to diminish my light.

Repeatedly, I broke the *Principles of Successful Alliances*. My innate power continued to try and lead me in the proper direction. I made powerful business connections with leaders within my industry, but my then husband did not want me to travel for work. I cut my ties with my contacts and went back to what was comfortable for him, but our marriage still failed. I had to learn not to share my dreams and my life with the wrong people, the distractors, the non-dreamers, and the non-doers.

Unwisely, I had been under the impression that if I supported people with their aspirations, then they would support me with mine. That was a fallacy. I had betrayed myself for far too many years. I had fantastic ideas and aspirations, but I had shared them with the wrong people. I had interfaced with hostiles on my journey. What I learned from those experiences was to only seek validation from myself and to push forward on my own mission. Those who could not support me were at a difficult point on their own journeys that had little to do with mine.

I wanted it all, and that was what I was going to attain. I began to work backwards. I balanced the needs and desires of life. I learned to say no and balance self in relation to others. My self-discipline soared. Nothing could knock me off of my game. Distractions fell by the wayside and opportunities and ideas opened as I progressed. Direction became even more evident in the mapping of my life.

I began to simplify my life, my schedule, my money, my time, my priorities, and my home. I tore through my house with a vengeance and got rid of all of the unnecessary clutter and paperwork, and created a peaceful home for my family and myself. As I did, things fell even more in place, and ideas flooded back into my mind.

The direction had been decided, I moved forward writing this book, but also gave myself a strict deadline. I calculated the exact number of days that I would allow to be taken away from my family for this endeavor and divided that into how many pages I anticipated the book would need. It really was that simple. I was sensitive to the fact that an imbalance would take place within my family's busy lives, so I limited that imbalance as much as I could. I made a conscious decision to believe in my competence and my ability to accomplish the task at hand. I pushed every doubting thought out of my mind and pushed forward with a fire in my belly.

The pressure of the deadline became my friend; I took on a calm excitement about fulfilling my destiny, which created endless power within my being. Human beings were made to create. Words and ideas came through me and kept coming until the end. I was anticipating a win, while at the same time planning the next correct move that would follow.

How do we check for success along our journey? How can we gauge a win? Things will feel right. Your internal knowing will speak to you. More opportunities will open, and the right people will come into your life. You will find a way to accomplish your goals, and when hurdles present themselves, you will jump over them or push them aside. You will become unstoppable. You will feel freedom in being your whole self and eager to learn more about whom that is to become. Create a map, get your bearings, and move forward with vigor.

MAP YOUR FINANCIAL GOALS

1.) _____

2.) _____

3.) _____

4.) _____

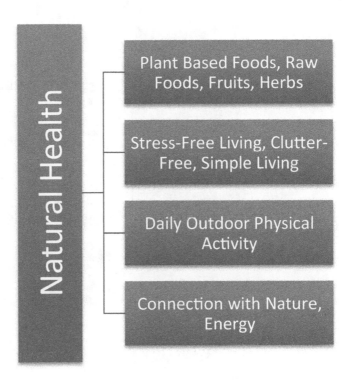

MAP YOUR HEALTH RELATED GOALS

1.) _____

2.) _____

3.) _____

4.) _____

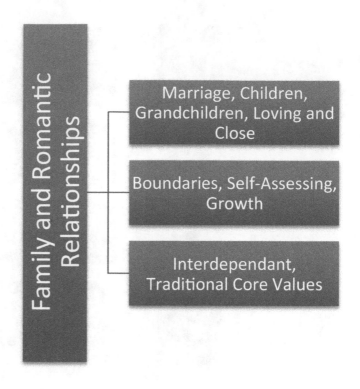

MAP YOUR RELATIONSHIP GOALS

1.) _____

2.) _____

3.) _____

4.) _____

Chapter 7

Leveling-Up Your Mission

Our potential is what happens when we make a conscious choice to go to our next level.

- Karen Berg

You have now acquired the *Principles and Mechanics* for winning at this game; how to care for yourself on your journey, attaining, retaining and growing *riches*, how to create *successful alliances* as well as discarding improper unions, vital ways to *increase your health*, as well as creating and *navigating the map* of your journey. Now it is time to share your gift with the world.

When you left the Creator to join the other players on this world, you were instilled with a special gift that no other being would possess. Now that you have learned how to navigate the external obstacles placed before you, your final mission is to dedicate the remainder of your journey to present your gift to those who are ready to receive it. Giving back to others is where your reward will be leveled-up by your drive and determination. At the completion of your mission, you will return to the Source to rejoin the other gods for reassignment.

Your arsenal is full of tools to navigate the quest ahead of you.

- Be mindful of the natural law of exchange; fine-tune your purpose of improving the lives of others.
- Develop through lifelong learning, share your wisdom and give to those who are competent allies.
- Complete the mission assigned to you before coming into this world. You will ripple on through history as the energy you create.

It feels so good to be alive and creating a win in this *omnipresent* journey. To get ahead in this game of life, question your current belief system, make a plan, follow the principles outlined in this guidebook, assess your progress, reassess your actions, and get ready for life's ups and downs. Strive to find a balance so you can stay the course. Spend the time learning how your choices have caused your current situation in life, as well as how your current actions are shaping the foreseeable future. Prepare with the winners, and anticipate a win. Give off that winning energy. Ride the energetic waves. Soar during the highs and regroup during the lows. Good or bad, you have created where you are right now.

It's time to make the next move...

Glossary

Due to the nature of the information contained within this book, I want you to have clear understanding of the word usage throughout. This glossary contains definitions both from the Merriam-Webster dictionary as well as clarifications from my view, which will help you grasp the full concept and meanings of the words.

acquisition – the act of acquiring something

agenda – an underlying often ideological plan or program

alliances – an association to further the common interests of the members (families, states, parties, or individuals)

allocate – to distribute for a specific purpose or to particular persons or things

allopathic – relating to or being a system of medicine that aims to combat disease by using remedies (such as drugs or surgery) which produce effects that are different from or incompatible with those of the disease being treated

analogy - a comparison of two otherwise unlike things based on resemblance of a particular aspect

apex – the highest or culminating point, a peak

arsenal - a collection of weapons

assess - to determine the importance, size, or value of something

avatar – an incarnation in human form

boundaries – something that indicates or fixes a limit or extent

chi - vital energy that is held to animate the body internally and is of central importance in some Eastern systems of medical treatment and of exercise or self-defense

collective consciousness – a term used to describe the practice of humans, and animals, sharing behaviors and ideas with each other subconsciously

compounding interest– interest computed on the sum of an original principal and accrued interest

construct – a created or false reality, a product of ideology, history, or social circumstances

consumerism - a preoccupation with and an inclination toward the buying of consumer goods

conventional mortgage loan – a home loan that is guaranteed by a private lender typically requiring a twenty percent down payment

convictions - a strong persuasion or belief

Creator – a higher power that brings something into existence

demise – a loss of position or status

depreciation - to lower the estimated value of

density – something to which a person or thing is predetermined

detoxification - to remove a harmful substance (such as a poison or toxin) or the effect of such from

distractors – one that distracts from a given course of action

diversified - to balance (an investment portfolio) defensively by dividing funds among securities of different industries or of different classes

duality – a doctrine that the universe is under the dominion of two opposing principles one of which is good and the other evil

ebb and flow – used to describe something that changes in a regular and repeated way

ego – the self especially as contrasted with another self or the world

emergency reserve – money saved in an easily accessible account used for unexpected expenses, equivalent to six months of income

emotional intelligence – the skill of identifying and managing your emotions and the emotions of others

entitlement - belief that one is deserving of or entitled to certain privileges

epiphany – an illuminating discovery, realization, or disclosure

equity – the money value of a property or of an interest in a property in excess of claims or liens against it

exponential - expressible or approximately expressible by an exponential function especially, characterized by or being an extremely rapid increase (as in size or extent)

facilitating – to make easier, help bring about

fallacy - a false or mistaken idea

fixed interest rate – a loan where the interest rate does not fluctuate during the period of the loan

fleece - to strip of money or property by fraud or extortion

fundamental - serving as a basis supporting existence or determining essential structure or function

game – a procedure or strategy for gaining an end

generic alteration (engineering) – the group of applied techniques of genetics and biotechnology used to cut up and join together genetic material and especially DNA from one or more species of organism and to introduce the result into an organism in order to change one or more of its characteristics

genetically modified organisms (GMO) – living organisms whose genetic material has been artificially manipulated through genetic engineering

herbalist - a person who practices healing by the use of herbs

heirarchy – the classification of a group of people according to ability or to economic, social, or professional standing

homeostasis - a relatively stable state of equilibrium or a tendency toward such a state between the different but interdependent elements or groups of elements of an organism, population, or group

impoverished – reduced to poverty

incentive - something that incites or has a tendency to incite to determination or action

inception – an act, process, or instance of beginning, commencement

innate – belonging to the essential nature of something, inherent

instant gratification – immediate satisfaction or pleasure

intentions – a determination to act in a certain way

investment broker – individuals who bring together buyers and sellers of investments

legacy - something transmitted by or received from an ancestor or predecessor or from the past

long term disability insurance - is an employee-paid benefit program designed to provide income replacement in the event you become disabled due to an illness or injury and cannot perform the duties of your normal job, or maybe any job, for a long period of time (6 months or longer)

manifest - readily perceived by the senses and especially by the sense of sight, to create

mind programming – the change of paradigms within the subconscious mind

monetarily - of or relating to money or to the mechanisms by which it is supplied to and circulates in the economy

natural laws – principles held to be derived from nature

novice – beginner

oblige – to constrain by physical, moral, or legal force or by the urgency of circumstance

obstacles – something that impedes progress or achievement

omnipresent - present in all places at all times

Originator – a higher power that creates or initiates something

pivotal – vitally important

portfolio – the securities held by an investor

Power of Attorney - a legal instrument authorizing one to act as the attorney or agent of the grantor

precautions – a measure taken beforehand to prevent harm or secure good

pre-tax salary (income) – earnings before taxes have been subtracted

principles - a rule or code of conduct

proactive – acting in anticipation of future problems, needs, or changes

proficient – well advanced in an art, occupation, or branch of knowledge

propaganda - ideas, facts, or allegations spread deliberately to further one's cause or to damage an opposing cause

psyche – soul, personality

prudent - shrewd in the management of practical affairs

purpose – something set up as an object or end to be attained

quagmire a difficult, precarious, or entrapping position

reactive - occurring as a result of stress or emotional upset

realm – sphere, domain

reassess – to assess (something) again

residual income – passive income occurring after all debts are paid from investments

rethinking – to engage in reconsideration

roll the dice – to take a chance on something

Roth 401k - is an employer-sponsored investment savings account that is funded with after-tax

savior – one that saves from danger or destruction

self-actualization - to realize fully one's potential

self-knowingness - having self-knowledge

sentient beings – finely sensitive in perception or feeling

serendipitous – the faculty or phenomenon of finding valuable or agreeable things not sought for

shill - one who acts as a decoy

short term disability insurance - refers to an injury or illness that keeps a person from working for a short time (less than 6 months)

status quo - the existing state of affairs within a society

strategy - the art of devising or employing plans toward a goal

source – obtained from a particular supernatural origin

subprime mortgage - having or being an interest rate that is higher than a prime rate and is extended chiefly to a borrower who has a poor credit rating or is judged to be a potentially high risk for default (as due to low income)

surmise – a thought or idea based on scanty evidence, conjecture

taboo – a prohibition imposed by social custom or as a protective measure

term life insurance – life insurance that pays a benefit in the event of the death of the insured during a specified amount of time (example: 20 years)

tinctures - a solution of a medicinal (HERBAL) substance in an alcoholic (OR GLYCERIN) solvent

traditional 401k - a retirement account to which employee and employer contribute, on which taxes are deferred until withdrawal, and for which the employee usually selects the types of investments

trajectory – a path, progression, or line of development resembling a physical trajectory

Trust - the legal relationship between one person (trustee), having an equitable ownership or management of certain property and another person (beneficiary), owning the legal title to that property.

Will - legal instrument that permits a person (testator), to make decisions on how his estate will be managed and distributed after his death

"Dictionary by Merriam-Webster: America's Most-Trusted Online Dictionary." *Merriam-Webster*, Merriam-Webster, 2018, www.merriam-webster.com/.

RETHINKING LIFE

The GUIDEBOOK for RECREATING YOUR LIFE and WINNING the GAME

About the Author

Michelle Laura Romero is an authority within the gaming and hospitality industries as well as a financial freedom educator, real estate expert, natural health and detoxification researcher, author, and speaker on applying the principles of wisdom to achieve winning outcomes. Basically, a math, science, psychology, and non-fiction geek!

www.**MichelleLauraRomero**.com